THE TRAVIS WALTON STORY BEGAN WITH A SINGLE, BIZARRE INCIDENT . . .

. . . a reported event so utterly fantastic that nobody possessed of sober and rational mind would believe it to be true. And yet, six witnesses testified to its apparent truth.

Thereafter came the deluge—bitter accusation and recrimination almost as unbelievable as the original event itself, a maelstrom of raging people flung about in a whirling storm of fear and confusion.

Thus, the Travis Walton story grew beyond itself, grew inexorably into the universal and eternal story of human action and reaction—an intense and diverse human drama, fraught with mystery and adventure and intrigue.

"The most cynical nonbeliever will be shaken by Bill Barry's account of the most intriguing UFO story to date."
—*Penthouse Magazine*

A faint internal rumble . . . he felt it was being aimed at the ranger station, and it sounded a scintillator.

ULTIMATE ENCOUNTER

The True Story
of a UFO Kidnapping

by

Bill Barry

A KANGAROO BOOK
PUBLISHED BY POCKET BOOKS NEW YORK

Another *Original* publication of POCKET BOOKS

The story upon which this book is based appeared in *Penthouse.*

POCKET BOOKS, a Simon & Schuster division of
GULF & WESTERN CORPORATION
1230 Avenue of the Americas, New York, N.Y. 10020

ISBN: 0-671-82079-6

First Pocket Books printing May, 1978

Trademarks registered in the United States and other countries.

Interior design by Sofia Grunfeld

Printed in the U.S.A.

There are more things in heaven and earth, Horatio,
than are dreamt of in your philosophy.

—Hamlet

Interesting, if true. . . . Interesting, anyway.
—Mark Twain

Knowledge is conceived from mystery, not explanation,
because mystery woos the mind to love what is as yet
unknown.

—O'Baire

Read not to contradict and confute, nor to believe and take for granted, but to weigh and consider.

—Francis Bacon

ULTIMATE
ENCOUNTER

1.

SOMETHING INCREDIBLE WAS ABOUT TO HAPPEN. DUSK was falling in the northern Arizona woods, and a November chill crept over the slate-colored earth.

It was Indian country, high up in the rocky timberlands of the Sitgreaves National Forest—a rugged, desolate, pinewood mountain range of primeval beauty . . . ancient home of the Apache and Navajo and Hopi, all of it steeped in misty centuries that echoed with sacred lore. The lore was handed down through generations by word of mouth. And it told of mysterious spirit-creatures who had journeyed earthward from the forever skies. They winged their way on engines of clouds that flashed. And sometimes they departed on ships of rock, with human warriors taken from the tribes.

Just over the ridgeline from the Fort Apache Indian Reservation, Mike Rogers was working on a Forest Service contract to thin out 1,277 acres of scrub brush at Turkey Springs. His six-man wood-cutting crew consisted of Travis Walton, Ken Peterson, John Goulette, Steve Pierce, Allen Dalis, and Dwayne Smith. Their job was to chop out all brush of less than six-inch trunk diameter. Three men cut with roaring chainsaws, and three followed behind, piling the debris for later burning.

Rogers supervised. He had been on this particular job for over a year, hiring men as he needed them. But on November 5, 1975, he was behind on his contract schedule, and he had already received one extension.

So the crew worked until last light, about six P.M. They were all young men, but they were bone-tired when they finally quit. Deep silence fell over the green pine woods.

11

The men loaded their saws into Rogers' 1964 crew-cab International truck, and then they climbed in for the ride home to Snowflake, a small Mormon settlement town forty miles north.

Rogers drove, with Peterson and Walton beside him on the front seat. The four others sat in the back, with the windows open to let their cigarette smoke out. The three in front were abstainers.

The truck wound slowly uphill, doing about four miles per hour over the hump-backed old logging road. The men bounced in their seats as the truck, dubbed Pogo, jounced along the rutted trail.

"Pogo is long overdue for some new shocks, boss," somebody wisecracked.

The night was clear and crisp, just dipping into the forties, with a little smell of winter in it. It was a fine night to go swimming in Snowflake's heated indoor community pool, Travis Walton said. How about it?

He had been sick the day before, mostly from carousing too much, and he had slept in the truck quite a bit that morning, trying to recover. Now, he said, he felt a lot better, and he wanted to go swimming. John Goulette said he was game. But Mike Rogers said that he was too damned tired to go swimming.

They had only gone about two hundred yards up the road toward the top of the rim when Allen Dalis leaned over from his back-seat window behind Walton and said, "What the hell is that out there?"

Mike thought Allen had seen a deer or something. They were passing a thicket of jack pines on the right. "There's a light glowing in there," Travis said.

At first glance it had looked like the sunset to him; but it was too bright to be the sunset, he thought. Steve Pierce guessed that it might be a crashed airplane hung up in the trees back there. The guys on the right side of the truck were all wondering aloud what it might be: maybe a hunter's camp, a cooking fire, somebody's headlights.

Mike didn't know what they were getting so excited about. He wasn't paying much attention to them, but as he steered the lurching truck around a right-hand bend in the road, somebody blurted out, "That's a UFO!" Around the bend, a clearing opened up in the woods to the right. Three slash piles (logging debris) sat in the clearing. The clearing was all lighted up. Suddenly, all the guys on the right side of the truck quit talking.

Then somebody shouted, "Stop the truck!"

Mike hit the brakes. Travis had already jumped out and was running into the clearing before the truck stopped. Mike switched off the engine and leaned over to his right to see out the window.

And there it was. A large glowing object was hovering fifteen to twenty feet above a slash pile, not one hundred feet away. It was so big that Mike couldn't see all of it through the windshield. But it looked just like a UFO is supposed to look.

Motionless and silent, it glowed a golden milky yellow, the color of hot molten iron when it comes out of the blast furnace. It appeared to be a solid structure, an oval, about twenty feet in diameter and eight feet from top to bottom. It had a milky white dome on top. The whole object was compartmented by dark, silvery, vertical lines—like window dividers, but no windows were visible. The compartments were longer than they were wide. A narrow band seemed to encircle the middle of the thing, an outer protruding rim that cojoined top and bottom at their widest circumference.

The UFO just hung there, silent and still, silhouetted against the black sky. A thirty-foot-tall pine tree rose up behind it, but well away from it, on the other side of the clearing.

In the first seconds, nobody said a word. They all stared dumbstruck by the glowing thing, not quite comprehending, not fully realizing. No lights were visible on the outside of the UFO. The glow seemed to be coming from within. It cast a golden milky light across the ground and into the trees, softly illuminating the forest. The UFO itself was an awesome thing, and it had a grandeur to it, awesomely perfect in some inexplicable way. But it also had a frightening aspect to it, eerie in its own glow, a muted glow and not dazzling or brilliant.

It took the men in the truck a few seconds to really understand what was happening. And, abruptly, Mike realized that Travis Walton was now walking directly to the slash pile, trying to get beneath the object. That looked like a very dangerous thing to do. So he hollered, "Hey! What the hell are you doing?"

Then the others yelled, "Travis! Get the hell away from there! Come back from there. . . !"

Travis always had to be the first one to bolt headlong into danger, always the first to take on anything, never scared.

Some of the men in the truck heard a slight beeping sound, like the warning bell on an airliner when the captain switches on the seat-belt sign. They were still yelling at Travis to come back from there.

He stopped at the slash pile. The object hung in the air above the other side of the pile. Unable to get closer, Travis stared up into its golden-glowing underside. It seemed utterly smooth, without ports or hatches, no bolts or rivets. It looked like a huge glowing light bulb. It was beeping.

And then it started to move. It began to wobble slowly, pitching and yawing on its axis. Then it made a loud noise, rumbling, as if it were coming alive.

Travis dropped to his knees, trying to hide behind a log sticking out of the slash pile. The men in the truck were terrified. Mike's heart was beating wildly against his chest.

The rumble grew louder, like a turbine generator winding up to full power, the sound of it rising in intensity. Rocking more swiftly, wobbling faster, smoothly gaining speed, it seemed as though the object were going to take off. It was like some great mechanical beast beating its wings, side to side, gathering power for flight, and it was all aglow with molten iron light.

Out of this movement, it uttered other sounds. All the sounds meshed together, rising to a chilling point until Mike could feel it more than he heard it. He felt it throbbing through the earth and the truck and himself. The throbbing sound that he could feel was what scared him more than anything.

The other guys were screaming at Travis to come back. Their voices were shrill and panicked. Travis turned his head, glanced back at them, gaped back at the object again, and he stood up. The thing was now making sounds like nothing any of the men had ever heard before.

Travis took a step. It looked to Mike like he was going to get the hell out of there. He caught the drift of his

14

own frenzied thoughts: *Something's happening to this thing, and it's a good idea Travis is getting out of there, and it looks like I'd better turn the truck on so we can get the hell out of here. . . .*

He reached down for the ignition, turning the key. Instantly, the thing yipped piercingly, and a flash of brilliant light blazed out across the ground and trees, blasting everything bluish-whitish-green. It burned his eyes, as if a bright flashbulb had gone off right in his face.

"It got him!" somebody screamed.

Peterson and Dalis saw a shaft of blue-green light shoot out of the object's bottom and hit Travis in the head and chest. He flew straight up, a foot off the ground, his whole body stiffened, his head thrown back, arms and legs flung out stiffly, and his whole body sharply outlined in blazing light. And he was hurtled backward through the air, stiff as a board and glowing, and he was banged into the ground ten feet away from where he had been standing, just as if an explosion had gone off in front of him. He lay there, flat on his back, not moving. It had all happened in a split second. The whole forest was lit up.

"Get the hell out of here!" the guys were screaming at Mike. "Get the hell out of here!" They thought the thing was shooting at them.

In blind panic, Mike had already hit the gas and mashed the pedal to the floor. The rattling truck careened up the road, bucking over the humps and ruts.

"It got him, it got him!" somebody was screaming. Pierce was wailing incoherently, like a wounded animal. Dalis scrambled around the back-seat floor, trying to hide. Somebody was praying aloud. Mike was just trying to get them out of there, fleeing in utter terror, so scared he could hardly see. His eyes were blurred, his fingers and feet were numb, and his stomach was all balled up with nausea flooding his gut.

The truck was flying along the hump-backed road, bouncing nearly out of control, missing trees by inches, racketing as if it were coming apart at every jar. Rocks tore into its underside as it skidded from side to side.

"Is the damned thing following us?" Mike yelled. All he could see in his rearview mirror was wildly bouncing light. He was sure the thing was right on their tail. But what was it going to do?

He had the accelerator floored, and he couldn't control the truck, couldn't even see the road. He was driving like a maniac to get away from *it*, oblivious to how he was driving, all a-lurch and smashing against tree limbs.

Suddenly a huge pine tree loomed up in the headlights. He swerved the wheel, braked, and the truck slid sideways. It came to a jolting halt, straddled crossways on a bulldozed-up mound of hard-packed dirt.

One of the guys screamed at him to keep going.

Mike turned his head to look back to where they had come from. They had only traveled about a quarter of a mile. He was ready to take off again if he got even a glimpse of it.

He couldn't see it. Nobody could see it. It wasn't following them. The forest was dark. The sky was dark. Everything was still and silent. Not even a flicker of glowing light showed through the trees. The woods closed in, pitch-black and soundless.

Just ahead was the Rim Road, the way out of the forest. Mike noticed that nobody in the truck was saying a word. They all just sat there, frozen, wordless, catatonic. The only sound was of Pierce crying. The UFO had been enough to scare them half to death, and the way Mike had been driving was enough to horrify them.

All of a sudden everybody started breaking loose. Steve Pierce went to pieces while the others climbed out of the truck, but he refused to get out. He stayed in the back seat, crying hysterically, refusing to respond to anything the others said to him.

Standing beside the truck, Allen Dalis was running his mouth at a hundred miles an hour, making absolutely no sense at all. The five men stood there in a bunch, yelling and screaming at each other. The forest resounded with their racketing hubbub, a flood of riotous words and screeches, complete hysterical turmoil, utterly confused and terrified.

Kenny Peterson had a blank, disbelieving look on his face. He was twenty-five, and with Mike, twenty-eight, they were the older, surer, most respected members of the crew. Pierce was only seventeen. Dwayne Smith was nineteen. Allen Dalis and John Goulette were both twenty-one.

Kenny Peterson finally said, "What the hell are we doing? Travis is still back there. Do you realize that we just ran off and left Travis back there? What happened to him? We just left him there."

And for the first time it dawned on Mike that that was exactly what they had done.

"It hurt him, I'm sure," he said. "He's still back there, hurt. We'll have to go back and get him."

Steve Pierce broke in for the first time from the truck.

"I ain't going back there," he sobbed. "Let's get out of here. Let's just get out of here . . . go to town and tell the sheriff. . . ."

Goulette and Smith agreed. No way they were going to go back there.

But Kenny insisted, "We have to go back and see what happened to him. We have to go back and get him."

"Well, you know, what about the UFO?" Mike said. "If we go back, we might get zapped ourselves."

For a few minutes they argued about what to do. They were getting a little calmer, a little more organized in their thoughts and speech.

Mike and Kenny finally made the decision: they were going back to get Travis.

"You guys who don't want to go back," Mike said, "can stay here."

"Oh, no," somebody said. "No way we're going to stay here alone."

Somebody suggested that they go tell someone, maybe get some guns, get some extra help and then go back. "We haven't got any guns—or anything. That thing will kill us."

As they were arguing, one of them glanced up to the Rim Road, about fifty feet away, and saw a camper go by. They had heard the hunters shooting in the woods all day. "Let's catch that camper," he said. "They can help us."

Not thinking how the camper might help them, they all started piling back into the truck. As he got to his door, Mike glanced back into the woods and saw a flash of light, just a white streak. It didn't get above the trees; it just seemed to streak through them, as if it had lifted straight up and *pffft!*—it was gone. He saw a streak and a blur of flashing light and then empty sky, total blackness.

"Hey, did you guys see that?" he yelled at them.

They didn't. They were all climbing into the truck. Now they clambered back out again and ran around to where Mike was standing.

"I'm sure that was it," he said, excited. "It just shot off into the sky. I didn't see all of it, just a streak as it went. I'm sure it's gone."

He wasn't sure at all. But he hoped he was right. What else could it have been? In a split second, it had disappeared toward the horizon.

But the others hadn't seen it. They kept looking, to see if anything like that would show again. But it didn't. Not a glimmer of light showed in the black sky.

They stood and talked about it for a few minutes. And Mike said, "Well, let's just go back." And a couple of the other guys then agreed that they would have to go back. "We can't just leave him there," Mike pressed them. "It looked to me like he was hurt—looked to me like he received some kind of injury. I don't know if it just stunned him, or hurt him, or what. But we've got to go back and look."

"Well, let's try to catch that camper first," somebody said.

"Yeah, we should get some help first," somebody else agreed.

So they all climbed back into the truck, and Mike drove it up onto the Rim Road, and they took off, chasing the camper. Of course, the camper was long gone. But Mike figured that maybe it would stop somewhere along the way. He didn't know what else to do. None of them really wanted to go back to the place alone.

They drove all the way to the Turkey Springs cutoff, but they didn't see anyone. So Mike turned the truck around and headed back toward the woods again. He was thinking that Travis was just lying there hurt, maybe even dead. He knew that they should have tried to help him. They should not have run, should not have left Travis alone.

They returned to the dirt road that wound down

through the woods. Mike stopped for about thirty seconds and they reconsidered the situation. Then they decided that it was okay, that the thing was probably gone, that they'd be all right, and it was safe to go on.

Mike started down the dirt road, going quite slowly now, three or four miles an hour, driving cautiously and watchfully. His heart was again pounding wildly in his chest. The others were quiet, still fearful.

After five minutes, they seemed to be in the right place, the right general area. It was hard to tell in the dark.

There were several clearings in which slash piles were stacked up. So they couldn't be sure that they were in exactly the right place. As they drove slowly by one spot, somebody said, "I think this is the place. This looks like it."

By then they had passed it. Mike stopped the truck and then backed up slowly. Kenny Peterson had taken the flashlight out of the glovebox. The clearing was now on Mike's left. He took the flashlight and shined it into the clearing.

Then he slowly nosed the truck in. The headlights hit right on a slash pile. "That's it," somebody said. "That's it."

Mike stopped the truck but left the engine running, and the headlights were shining right on the slash pile. There was no sign of the UFO. There was no sign of Travis. Mike shined the flashlight around the ground. Nothing. Then he gave the light to Kenny and he flashed it around. Still nothing.

They sat dazed and silent for a moment. Then Mike said, "Okay, we need to get out and look around."

Nobody moved. They started arguing all over again. Steve was shaking, and he said he wouldn't get out. "All right," Mike said. "Stay in the truck." But no, he didn't want to do that, either; he wouldn't stay in the truck alone.

Finally, Mike opened his door and got out. So the others got out, too.

"It's best if we all stick in a group," Mike said, and they all agreed to that.

All of them were scared. It was very dark outside the glare of the headlights and very silent, with the eerie feel of the deep, shadowy woods closing in on them. They didn't know what they would find, or what would find them.

Mike's eyes were still blurred, so he couldn't see too well. He felt numb and nauseated and sick. The other guys said they felt the same way—scared, numb, half sick, panicky.

Staying very close together, touching, they walked slowly around the slash pile, shining the single flashlight over the ground. Then they circled out a little bit farther, sure that Travis was right there, somewhere close. Still, they didn't find him. There was nothing there. So they circled out wider to the next slash pile, and back around by the truck, and then on to the next slash pile, going all around that.

They didn't find anything—no blood, no tracks, no clothing. Nothing. There was not a trace of Travis. Mike was sure that the first slash pile was where they had last seen Travis.

They were trying to stay within the lights of the truck, within sight of the truck. After twenty minutes they had searched all over the top of the ridge, staying close together, and they had circled back down again to the truck. They had found nothing.

The realization started to hit them that Travis was gone, perhaps having stumbled off alone hurt into the woods, or what else, they didn't know. He just wasn't there.

A couple of guys started crying. Then Mike started to cry, not bawling, but weeping very softly. He fell to his knees. Travis was his best friend. He was bewildered, frightened, scared of what might have happened to his friend, and maybe a little ashamed.

It was all too much for him to handle. It was too much for all of them. They couldn't understand it. It was too bizarre, unthinkable, unreal. Their heads were whirling with the oncoming realization of what had happened.

It couldn't have happened. And, yet, it did. But at the same time, they didn't really know what had happened.

It had all been so quick and their perceptions of it were so terror-stricken. They didn't know what to think, didn't know what to believe.

"Well, he's not here," Mike finally said. "He's just not here. We'd better drive out to Heber and call the sheriff."

2.

IT WAS A TEN-MILE DRIVE OUT OF THE WOODS TO HEBER, a small mountain junction town straddling the main highway out of Payson, Route 260.

At Heber, Junction 277 wends northeast to Snowflake; Route 260 dips southeast to Show Low, Lakeside, and Pinetop.

The resident Navajo County deputy sheriff in Heber was Chuck Ellison. About seven-forty-five that night, the telephone rang in his home and he answered. An excited voice on the other end of the line said he was Kenny Peterson, calling from one of the phone booths at the Wilbur Shopping Center in town. There were six of them there, from Mike Rogers' thinning crew, and they needed help.

They wanted Deputy Ellison to come over and talk to them right away. It was a matter of great urgency.

"Well, what's wrong?" Ellison asked.

"One of our men is missing in the woods, and we need help right away."

Ellison left the house and drove over to the phone booths at Wilbur's. Mike Rogers' crew was waiting for him. They told him what had happened. They had encountered a UFO in the woods near Turkey Springs, and it looked to them as if it had picked up Travis Walton. He was gone; they couldn't find him.

All six men were highly agitated. Two of them were crying. *If they're lying,* Ellison thought, *they're damned good actors.*

He decided that he'd better alert the sheriff in Holbrook, forty miles north. Navajo County Sheriff Marlin

Gillespie listened to Ellison's story and told him to wait with the crew right where they were. He hurried down to Heber with his under-sheriff, Ken Coplan.

The witnesses repeated their story. All of them were upset. They all told the same story. Gillespie didn't know what to think about it. Certainly it was incredible, but he himself had had some unusual experiences with so-called UFOs. Therefore, he was not one to dismiss the idea of them automatically. Still, he had his doubts about this yarn. A man snatched up by a UFO, kidnapped—that was a bit too much.

"Well," he said, "we'd better go back there and have another look."

Pierce, Smith, and Goulette flatly refused to return to the woods. So they drove Mike's truck home to Snowflake and told his wife what had happened.

The rest of the crew took the sheriff and his deputies back to where they claimed to have confronted the UFO. Mike suggested that they call in somebody with bloodhounds—the dogs would follow wherever Travis' tracks led, if he had wandered off hurt, not knowing what he was doing. Or the dogs would take the scent to the slash pile and stop, unable to track the scent any farther.

Instead, they made a search with flashlights and a four-wheel-drive Jeep mounted with a searchlight. As far as the sheriff's men were concerned, they were simply looking for a missing person. Their immediate investigation was focused on finding Travis Walton, or uncovering some clue to indicate what had happened to him.

Not finding anything at the clearing, the searchers widened out, looking for tracks. Most of the ground was shale and rock, not the best place for tracking footprints —if any were there to be tracked.

Deputy Ellison made a very thorough and close inspection of the clearing itself. Though it was dark and he was working by flashlight, he could find no evidence that a struggle of any kind had occurred on the ground. There were no signs of scuffling, no broken twigs, and no trampled or crushed beds of pine needles. He traced the path from where the crew's truck had been to the slash pile over which the UFO had allegedly appeared, and he did not find any prints from Travis Walton's distinctly shod work boots.

Most significantly, he thought, he did not find any burn spots at the slash pile, on the dry tindery ground, or on any of the surrounding trees. In fact, he could not find any indication that anything at all had been in that place recently—not a clue to show that either Travis Walton or a UFO had ever been there.

After conferring with Sheriff Gillespie, Ellison returned to Heber, notified additional deputies and members of the local volunteer posse association, and they all met at the scene to continue the search that night.

Mainly, the men were looking for tracks—on the dirt logging roads, or any place where there was loose dirt on which footprints would leave their impression.

Down toward the lower end of the wooded basin, a set of tracks was located. Several deputies converged, and hunkered down to inspect the prints by flashlight.

"They're cold," one of the men said. He seemed to know a few things about tracking. "They're at least a day old, maybe more. Couldn't be his."

Mike Rogers looked them over, and he shook his head, no. "That's not the kind of boot he was wearing. They aren't his tracks."

Also, the tracks seemed to split off in two directions, one trail leading up the ridgeline, the other going downhill toward the lower basin.

Somewhat disappointed, the searchers shook their heads. No, the tracks did not belong to Travis Walton.

By midnight they had found no trace of him at all.

Finally, Mike Rogers said, "We'd better tell his mother."

Mary Walton Kellet was staying at an isolated ranch in Bear Springs, ten to eleven miles east in the woods. Usually, she moved out there for the hot mountain summers, then returned to her brick home in Snowflake just before winter set in.

Mike and Deputy Ken Coplan drove over to the ranch to tell her the news. It was nearly one o'clock in the morning, and she was alone in the wood-frame cabin. As far as Mary Walton Kellet knew, there was nobody around for miles, so when she heard the car drive up, she went to the door with a gun.

Although she didn't recognize the car, she had known Mike for many years. As he passed in front of the headlights, she could see that he was very upset. That was not like Mike. Normally, he was calm and equable, a strong-willed and imperturbable young man. Now his whole appearance sagged, weighted by some great stress. Something was wrong.

Mary Walton Kellet opened the back door and said, "Mike, I don't know who you're with, but would you mind having him move over into the light? I'd like to know who I'm talking to."

The other man moved into the glare of the headlights and identified himself as Deputy Sheriff Ken Coplan.

"Is it all right if we come in?" Mike asked.

She replied, "Why, yes." She showed them in. Since there was no electricity that far out in the back country, she pumped up the Coleman lantern and lit it.

Then Mike asked her, "Have you seen Travis?"

"Well, not since I was in town a few days ago. Why?"

"I've got something to tell you," Mike answered. "He disappeared."

"*Disappeared?* What do you mean, disappeared?"

Mike looked like he was about ready to have a nervous breakdown. The features on his handsome face fidgeted, and his pale blue eyes were stricken with his anguish.

He told her the story. Then she had him tell it to her again, trying to get it straight in her own mind. From what she could grasp, they were coming out of the woods when they saw this object. Travis jumped out of the truck to get a better look. And, whatever the thing was, it sent out a beam of light, or a ray, and it hit Travis in the face or chest. They weren't certain because his back was turned to them. He hit the ground and they drove off in fright. It looked to them like he was down and hurt. But when they finally went back to retrieve him, he wasn't there. He was gone. And the UFO was gone.

She stood there in the flickering lantern light, staring at Mike, and she held herself together. She would not go to pieces.

Deputy Coplan didn't like her reaction; rather, he didn't like her *lack* of reaction. She seemed to be taking the news much too calmly. She didn't cry, wail, scream —nothing. She showed no visible reaction at all. And that just looked plainly suspicious to him.

A mother who has just been told that her son might have been abducted by aliens from outer space ought to be fretting and fussing all over the place. That's what he thought.

"Have you told anyone else?" she asked.

"No," Mike answered, "none of the family. Just the people out there looking for him now are all who know."

"Well," she said, "I guess I'd better go to town and tell the rest of the children."

The deputy drove off in his car to report back to the sheriff. He sure didn't like what he had seen. Mike drove her to town in her pickup, because she couldn't drive at night. She had night blindness, seeing rows of lights where only one row existed.

But, at fifty-seven, Mary Walton Kellet was a remarkable woman. Had Coplan known more about her, his initial impression of her might have been altered considerably. Instead, he reported to Sheriff Gillespie that the mother's reaction just didn't look right to him. Something was wrong here, he was sure. She didn't even ask to be taken to the scene. Very matter-of-fact about the whole thing, she simply said that she was going to town to tell the rest of the children that Travis had been snatched by a UFO.

There were six children, all grown. Travis was twenty-two. His younger brother, the baby, was in the army. After their parents had separated, the burden of raising and caring for six children had fallen to Mary. To support them, she had operated a twenty-one-room boardinghouse and an answering service in Phoenix. She had learned over the years that when there is only one parent, you can't afford to go to pieces when one of the children gets hurt. You hang on to everything until the situation is under control and the hurt child is under a doctor's care. Then you go quietly into a corner somewhere and fall apart . . . at least that's what she did.

After her own children were grown, she started raising five foster children—three Apache sisters and two brothers from another family. But illness struck her down, Chalmer's Flu, a killer, and it had left her partially crippled. She was small, dark-haired, and wiry, and she was part Indian. Her father had been one-quarter Cherokee and Welsh; her mother had been a red-haired Irishwoman. The older she herself got, the more Cherokee she seemed to become. Stoic in the face of trouble, as strong in spirit as any of the mountain men, she was a doer, not a crier. Hysterics only got in the way of doing what needed to be done.

Later on in private, she'd cry a little. But she'd never show her emotions to a stranger, never—not if she could help it, anyway. Instead, she'd take her tranquilizers and hang on to her nerves.

Had Deputy Coplan only asked her why she wasn't falling apart with the news she'd been told, she would have told him, "I'm like this—you share good news, and nobody has to ask you. But grief, or when you're upset, you keep it to yourself. That's the Indian in me. I'm very quiet about things like this. I just don't see that my going to pieces, when my children would be upset, would help anybody. I don't show my emotions to a stranger. I try to get something done about the problem at hand."

Besides, she had had a forewarning that something was going to happen to Travis. At six-fifteen that evening, alone in the ranch cabin, she had started to feel that old nervous twist in her stomach. She began to pace up and down, faster, and to smoke continuously. Her mind had suddenly seized upon Travis; she didn't know why. She just knew that something had gone wrong with him, that he was in trouble, in danger. She couldn't visualize the specific danger, as she sometimes did when one of her kin was in peril. Sometimes she visualized clearly what the danger was, without knowing who was endangered.

But at six-fifteen that evening, she knew it was Travis who was in trouble, though she didn't know what the trouble was.

It was just about six-fifteen when Travis bolted from the moving truck and ran toward the flying saucer while the six other wood-cutters watched, screaming at him in rising horror.

Mike drove her to her daughter's home in Taylor, a hamlet just outside Snowflake. Allison was very close to her brother. She broke down crying when she heard the story. Then she went into the bedroom and woke up her husband, Grant Neff.

"Well," Mary told them, "I'd better call Duane and tell him."

Duane lived in Glendale, a west-side suburb of Phoenix. Next to Don, Duane was the oldest son, and the strongest, physically and emotionally. In times of trouble, he was the head of the fatherless family.

About three o'clock in the morning, the phone rang in his house. It rang for quite a while, finally awakening Duane's wife, Carol. Duane was still dreaming. "Carol, answer the phone," he mumbled. "I'm talking to Travis."

All of Mary's boys were like that. When they went to sleep, they just died. But they'd carry on a conversation, just as if they were awake. They'd always been that way, even when they were little. She could talk to them when they were asleep, and they'd talk right back to her.

So when Duane told Carol that he was talking to Travis, she shook her head knowingly and answered the telephone. In a minute she yanked him awake, saying, "Duane, you'd better wake up. It's your mother."

Her voice was excited, and it was after three A.M, so he knew something was wrong. His mother told him exactly what Mike Rogers and Deputy Coplan had told her.

"Mother," he said, "I'll be there quick as I can make it."

Minutes later, Duane was wide awake and driving hard for Snowflake, two hundred miles away.

It is a rugged drive up—through the empty valley desert, which finally cuts upward into the craggy rocky buttes, then climbs ever higher into thick-forested timber country. The road snakes over hairpin curves, falling rock zones slashing down to the highway on one side, long, precipitous straight-down mountain plunges on the other. In the dark of night, it is a dangerous journey, made only more hazardous by frantic speed.

The route runs right through Heber, then finally emerges onto the high plateau named Mogollon—a frontier of vast, rolling, rangetop prairie that is harsh, isolated, and brooding, both beautiful and stark. The elevation pops the ears at six thousand feet. On a clear night, you can see endlessly across the vast unobstructed skies. They are skies in which the people there have watched strange and mysterious lights for years.

27

Snowflake is a small, dust-blown, *Last-Picture-Show* town. It was founded in 1878 by wandering Mormon settlers, as was its next-door neighbor, Taylor, named for John Taylor, president of the Mormon Church. Mormon apostle Erastus Snow named Snowflake after himself and his fellow Mormon pioneer, William J. Flake.

The Flake family retains strong influence in the town, for it is a place still largely populated by the descendants of the original settlers. Many of the old ways still prevail; many of the original lines of power remain intact.

The town marshal is Sanford (Sank) Flake. The resident Navajo County deputy sheriff is his brother, Glen Flake, who has also served as the sheriff. The Flake families control ranches, The Emporium, a western department store, The Feedbag restaurant, and a few other holdings in the town, which is only five blocks long from the railroad tracks to the end of Main Street. Main Street then becomes Route 77 north to Holbrook, the county seat, and it turns south into Route 277, which goes to Heber.

In the middle of town, one full square block is occupied by the awesome Mormon Church of Jesus Christ of Latter-Day Saints. It is an imposing, sprawling building, hewn from huge slabs of coppery-tinted stone blocks. It is an edifice that would be impressive anywhere. In Snowflake, it is all the more impressive for its sharp contrast to the surrounding town: small, low houses built of clapboard and brick, tiny stores, a few gas stations, the Cedar Motel, and three bars on outlying roads.

Just a spit away from the church sprawls the town's biggest business—the Snowflake Union (Regional) High School and Elementary School campus, composed of classroom buildings, the gymnasium, auditorium, activity centers, and the stadium, Home of the Lobos—all of it spread across a commanding hill.

A block off Main Street, cattle graze on front lawns. It is farm country, and horse country, and cow country. Pigpens and chicken coops squat hard by plain homes that look out comfortably at the rolling lands of the nearby countryside on which are scattered some twenty-five hundred people.

South of town, there is a feed-and-grain mill. West,

there is a paper mill. North and east are rocky hills grizzled with sagebrush.

The people are hardy, simple, and God-fearing. They believe in the Constitution and education and right-from-wrong. The men wear cowboy hats and cowboy boots. Evenings, the kids drive pickups back and forth on the darkened main drag. The next large towns are thirty and forty miles away, along America's last frontier.

By ten o'clock, Snowflake slumbers, deserted, dark. On wintry nights, the slicing wind whistles across the bare pasture earth, chilling the last of the graybeard grasses. Woodsmoke curls up its burning odors from every chimney. And very late, the baleful wail of a southbound freight train echoes through the deep silence.

It is a lonely place.

True to his word, Duane Walton arrived before daybreak, and he took charge of his family.

It was not a time that he would ever look back on with fondness. It was a bitter time, a taxing time, an angry time, a time of great and lingering pain for many and diverse people, flung together and clashing—whether by pure fate, or by the hand of human machination, or by both.

3.

As usual, Forest Service Sales Administrator Junior Williams reported for work at the Overguard Ranger Station at eight o'clock in the morning. The chief ranger had gathered a dozen or so Forest Service people together and had informed them that there would be a change in the normal routine.

The sheriff was organizing a manhunt in the Turkey Springs area, and they would join the sheriff's deputies, members of the Navajo County and Silver Creek sheriffs' posses, and search for a missing man whose name was Travis Walton. No more particulars were given.

"You are to meet Deputy Sheriff Chuck Ellison at Heber," the ranger said, "and he'll fill you in there."

They met Ellison at Heber. About two dozen other searchers joined them, and without any further briefing, Ellison formed them all into a convoy. They traveled down to the head of Turkey Springs to await the arrival of Sheriff Marlin Gillespie.

At this point, all Junior Williams knew about the situation was that Travis Walton had been missing since the night before. He was aware that Walton had been working for Mike Rogers on the Forest Service's thinning contract. And he just assumed that Walton had gotten separated from the rest of the crew and they hadn't been able to find him the previous night.

About half an hour later, four or five cars came tearing past the search party, went down into the ditch line, and disappeared into the woods, leaving only a rising cloud of dust behind them.

Williams couldn't imagine what the devil was going on here.

Then someone said, "That's Mike Rogers' work crew."

Right after that, the sheriff arrived, and they all proceeded on to the first ridge east of Turkey Springs. Mike Rogers was there, so Junior Williams walked over to him and struck up a conversation, getting right to the point.

"When did you last see him?" he asked. Then, "Exactly where did you see him last? What was he doing that he got lost from the rest of you?"

Rogers gave him a real odd look, startled, and said, "Well, haven't you heard?"

"Heard what?"

"You'll never believe this as long as you live, but we saw a UFO last night, and it picked him up."

Williams was flabbergasted. He'd known Mike for some time, through their mutual dealings with the Forest Service's slash-lopping program. In fact, he was Mike's contract supervisor, and he considered Mike a good, sound, level-headed young man. Williams both liked and respected him. Mike was having a little bit of trouble completing this particular contract on time, but it was nothing serious. An inspection of the work was scheduled within the next few days so that payment could be made for the job to date. Williams didn't forsee any problems.

But now, as Mike told him the rest of the story, Williams stared at him with considerable astonishment. He could see that Mike was really distraught, badly upset. He seemed even to be in a state of shock. That was not at all like the Mike Rogers he knew.

Meanwhile, Sheriff Gillespie had begun to have dark thoughts about what might have really happened to Travis Walton. He and Deputy Ellison discussed the possibility that there had been a fight amongst the crew. Travis might have been killed, then buried, and the UFO story could have been concocted to hide what had actually happened.

So Gillespie had called his Snowflake deputy, Glen Flake, on the dispatch radio and had asked him about these boys. Flake said yes, he knew most of them quite well. He knew Travis and Mike and Kenny Peterson especially well.

"Would you believe what they told you?" Gillespie asked.

"Why, yes, I think so—Mike and Kenny, certainly."

"Call me on the telephone," Gillespie said.

Flake did. Gillespie told him the whole story. The boys were saying that Travis had been taken by a UFO. Well, doubts did begin to creep into Glen Flake's mind. Grown men don't believe that kind of story.

So he also drove out to the search site that morning.

From the work crew, only Mike, Allen Dalis, and Kenny Peterson were there. The others still refused to return. The crew pointed out the clearing with the three slash piles in it, and they verified that that was the place. They were pretty certain that was where the UFO had been.

The sheriff formed a person-near-person combing line of men and they began to spread out over the area. The land ran along a very hard, rocky ridge, and it was in reproduction with a heavy stand of young pines.

Williams noted that the dead brush pile was at least a year old. The needles were dry, thickly carpeting the ground. If there had been a fire of any kind there, the whole place would have ignited immediately. He figured that an ordinary house match could have set the whole place ablaze, let alone the fiery blast of a departing spaceship. He assumed that was how a spaceship would take off, just like the rockets that blasted off in the space shots at Cape Kennedy.

Like Ellison, he noticed no broken limbs, no crushed needles, no burn spots, no pod prints—nothing to indicate that anything had ever been there. By now, Ellison was looking for ground marks far more sinister than footprints. He was looking for any sign of broken earth, any place where the hard ground had been hacked open, where a body might have been dumped in, then shoveled over again with dirt and brush.

Glen Flake was teamed with Kenny Peterson, searching up on the ridge. Flake was a slow-looking, stocky man with close-cropped gray hair. But he was a bright man, whose placid blue eyes belied his quick intelligence, till they twinkled up with sly wit.

He was trying to kid Kenny out of the UFO story, goading him with, "Where'd you hide the body, heh, Kenny?

C'mon, you can tell me. I know you didn't do it. You just tell me and we'll all get out of here, go home, and get some rest."

Flake kept at him, but Kenny was just as serious as a hen laying an egg. He didn't want to kid about it. He was definitely looking for the missing man. He really thought a UFO had zapped Travis. He believed that Travis was either stumbling around out there hurt, or that he had been carried off by the UFO.

Of all the boys, Kenny was the one Flake had to believe. Kenny always went to church. He didn't drink, or smoke, or run wild at all. He was a serious, sincere, honest boy. And Glen Flake had to believe that Kenny truly believed what he said had happened.

Furthermore, it was pointless for Flake to tell himself that he didn't believe in the existence of UFOs. He'd seen them himself. His family had seen them. Many people around Snowflake had seen them. They didn't claim to know what they were. They didn't claim that they were spacecraft from other planets. They were just unexplained lights, movements, objects in the sky. UFOs. By definition, that's what they were—Unidentified Flying Objects.

They'd be going low, then stop maybe half a mile away from an observer, then shoot off at crazy angles, at crazy speeds. It would be ridiculous for people to say that they hadn't seen them when they had. They weren't planes, not stars, not anything people were used to seeing. They were not normal lights and movements and objects in the sky.

Glen Flake just didn't know what they were. But he certainly knew that they existed. And so did a lot of other people up on the high plateau.

But to believe that Travis Walton had been grabbed by one and toted off into the sky—that was a whole different pot of stew. Flake didn't know if he could believe that, especially since it was Travis Walton who was gone.

The search had fanned out from the clearing, with forty to fifty men on foot scouring a radius of a mile or so. No trace of Travis Walton was found. Around eleven o'clock, someone suggested that a radiation test be made of the clearing where the UFO had reportedly appeared. A Civil Defense radiation monitoring system was maintained at the ranger station, and it included a scintillator, a measuring device even more sensitive than a Geiger counter.

Junior Williams radioed for it and it was brought out to the site. To determine if it was operating properly, it was checked against several luminous watch dials. Their radiation count was three.

The ground and slash pile each measured only one and a half.

Though Mike Rogers and Allen Dalis had bathed and changed their clothes since the alleged UFO encounter, the ranger checked them over with the scintillator and got only a slight reading. Certainly not harmful, he said, and probably not even unusual. Their hard hats, however, measured six. But the ranger refused to check Mike's truck, and a minor spat broke out over his refusal.

Goaded by quick-spreading rumor and gossip, some of the searchers were openly contemptuous toward the UFO story. And the general attitude of disbelief derived largely from the unsubstantiated opinions of certain deputy sheriffs who did not mind telling people what they thought.

It had been seventeen to eighteen hours since the UFO had allegedly appeared in the area, perhaps time enough for radiation to disperse—assuming that a real UFO would, in fact, leave radiation behind. All in all, the sheriff and the ranger agreed that there was no unusual radiation in the area, and they frankly didn't believe that the passage of time was responsible. Neither was an expert on either radiation or UFOs.

A brief check for unusual magnetism was then made with an ordinary field compass. The area had no affect on the magnetized compass needle.

Another combing foot search was made, widening out over a two- to three-square-mile area. Meanwhile, Mary Walton Kellet and her son Duane arrived on the scene. When the second sweep through the woods also failed to produce any trace of Travis, word spread that Mary Walton Kellet said that she didn't think there was any use in looking for him anymore, because he just wasn't there.

Mindful of Deputy Coplan's report about the mother's unemotional reaction to her son's disappearance, Deputy Ellison now also thought that she was reacting very matter-of-factly to the situation. From what other people were saying, and from listening to her, he got the impression that she had expected this to happen at any time . . . and whenever *they* got done checking him out, *they*'d bring him back just fine. In Ellison's view, she seemed to think that her son just wasn't on this earth anymore, so she didn't feel that keeping everyone out there looking for him would solve anything.

Ellison agreed with Coplan: the mother's behavior seemed suspicious. And Junior Williams agreed with both of them. He couldn't understand why Mary and Duane seemed to be treating the incident so calmly. Reportedly, she had said, "Well, I know he's with *them*. I know he's all right." The very idea struck Williams as being too weird to be real. He thought the mother was acting like a person no more stirred up than if her son had gone off to Show Low with some friends. For an incident of this magnitude, he thought, both the mother and her older son were taking it too calmly. He didn't think either one of them was reacting in a normal way. To his way of thinking, they should have been expressing more concern, showing more panic.

But running it all through his mind, he honestly didn't know what to believe. He found it pretty hard to be a fifty-year-old man tromping through the woods looking for someone who had been zapped by a UFO. He had heard UFO stories all his life, and he had always tried to keep an open mind about them. But when it came this close to him, he found it pretty hard to remain calm and reasonable. It was just too close to home to swallow whole-hog. Still, he had tried to believe in UFOs because there had been too many stories about them flying around. And, as many sightings as there had been, he thought that there was bound to be some truth in some of the stories. They weren't all publicity gimmicks. But he also believed that Mary and her son were acting strange, from what he could see and also from what he had heard about them. There were stories going around that they used to watch these things out at their Bear Springs ranch, that maybe one of them had contacted UFOs before, that UFOs had chased one of them, and that Travis had said that if he ever saw another one again, he would try to make contact with it.

All of it sounded very strange to Junior Williams,

though he had no idea how much of the gossip was actually true.

But as well as he knew Mike Rogers, he definitely believed that Mike was in a state of shock over whatever had happened. He definitely thought that those other boys had seen something that was extraordinary enough to scare the pants off them. But he couldn't say for sure what they had seen.

He was just a little bit nagged by the possibility that they had seen exactly what they said they had seen. And that was a pretty scary prospect.

In the afternoon, Sheriff Gillespie called in all the searchers and told them that his deputies would take over; the rest of them were free to go. The sheriff was nobody's fool. He didn't know what was going on here, but he intended to find out, in his own way.

Just like Travis' mother, he also didn't think there was any use in searching further—not without more information, or some new lead to justify keeping all these men away from their regular jobs just to tramp around out there over territory that had already been covered four and five times.

He had nothing to go on except the stories of the six witnesses.

A few miles to the west of the site, the Forest Service maintained the Gentry Fire-Watch Tower. It had been manned on the day Travis Walton disappeared. Surely if a brightly lit object had been flying around the woods, the fire-watcher should have seen it. But when a check of the tower was made, the sheriff learned that the watcher had gone off duty at five P.M., an hour and fifteen minutes before the UFO allegedly appeared to Mike Rogers' crew.

So the sheriff had nothing to go on beyond what Rogers' crew told him.

For the rest of that day, and the next, he kept a few deputies out in the search area. Officially, he listed the case as a missing-person investigation. So far it had created no undue interest or excitement, except for those close at hand.

However, on Saturday, the third day of the disappearance, all hell broke loose. Sheriff Gillespie had visitors at his office in Holbrook—Mike Rogers and Duane Walton. They had been to the search area and discovered that no one, absolutely no one, was out there looking for Travis Walton.

Duane was hot-mad. He was six-foot-three, about two hundred forty pounds, a professional boxer, a rodeo bull-rider, a professional horse-shoer, he didn't drink or smoke, and he took college courses on the side. He was an imposing and impressive man. Though some people thought him pushy and something of a kook, he was not a man to be trifled with. He wanted some action out there in the Turkey Springs woods, and he wanted it now.

A full-scale search was resumed Saturday—men on foot, men on horses, men in four-wheel-drive Jeeps. Saturday afternoon, a helicopter was also brought in to survey the area from the air. Since Duane had had military helicopter experience overseas, he went aloft as a spotter.

And, by Saturday, also, word of the incredible story had leaked to the outside world. News reporters and independent UFO investigators descended on the area. One of the first outside investigators to arrive was Fred Sylvanus, director of the Arizona Regional UFO Project, based in Phoenix, which, with Tucson, headquartered a number of respected UFO experts and organizations.

Sylvanus was a twenty-year veteran field investigator for all the major national UFO organizations. A short, bespectacled, probing man, he threw himself into the Walton case with a zest belying his nearly seventy years.

Late Saturday, almost exactly seventy-two hours after Travis Walton had disappeared, Sylvanus was interviewing Mike Rogers, with Duane Walton sitting in as an observer. They were in Sylvanus' Volkswagen van, equipped with a tape recorder. Sylvanus used such tapes in an adult education course he taught at a Phoenix college. Duane kept interrupting Mike's narrative of events, and that was beginning to irritate Sylvanus, who feared that the tape recording of the session would fast become too much of a hodgepodge for use in his class.

Mike described what had happened the previous Wednesday. He became especially engrossed in describing the UFO. "It was really kind of pretty. It had really smooth lines to it, and the coloration was really pretty the way it was glowing; it had kind of a milky, reddish-white look. And it was kind of pretty, you know, like a fancy new car. . . . The thing that impressed me most about it was that it was really beautiful. It looked natural, some-how—it looked good, like a Corvette, like a nice-looking new car. It had a nice color, and it was glowing, not so bright that you couldn't see it. It was just bright enough so you could see it, and it looked good."

Duane interrupted. "Nothing to horrify, just esthetically pleasing to the eye."

"Yeah," Mike answered.

"I might interrupt this with something," Duane inter-jected. "I saw one almost identical to what they described, for a period of about thirty minutes, in broad daylight, about twelve years ago, at one o'clock in the afternoon, about eight miles from this location right here. And it fol-lowed me around these woods for about thirty minutes, and it was never more than two hundred feet from me at any time. The picture they have drawn is almost identi-cal to what I saw, but without the [compartmented] lines. . . ."

"It may be the difference in seeing it in the day, instead of night," Mike offered. Meanwhile, alarms were going off in Sylvanus' head, warnings.

"It was just eight miles down this particular dirt road right here," Duane added.

"After Travis jumped out of the truck and I got it stopped . . ." Mike began to say.

"Again, let me interrupt," Duane said. "Travis and I discussed this many, many times at great length. . . . We both said that we would immediately get as directly under the object as was physically possible. We discussed this time and time again. The opportunity would be too great to pass up, and at any cost, except death, we were to make contact with them. And whoever happened to be left on the ground—if one of us didn't make the grade—would try to convince whoever was in the craft to come back and get the other one. But he performed just as we said we would, and he got directly under the object, and he's received the benefits for it."

"You hope he has," Mike said.

Duane's rapidly blurted statements were a revelation to Sylvanus. They disclosed strong previous interest in UFOs, perhaps even a preoccupation. Such interest usu-ally forewarned of tainted stories. The veteran UFO in-vestigator smelled a rat. He had not anticipated the admission. He now wanted to see how far Duane would go with it.

Mike continued his story. When he recounted the part about the crew finally returning to the slash pile, he said, "There wasn't a trace of him. There wasn't any blood, no markings on the ground, no burned places, no broken branches—there wasn't any evidence that anything had ever been there. I wish there would have been. I wish there would have been three big old burn places, like I'd heard about, like these mutilations that have been happening right up here in Pinetop and McNary. . . ."

Sylvanus did not ask what mutilations Mike was referring to.

"We never saw the thing set down," Mike continued. "That may be why there weren't any marks. . . . We don't know that he was picked up by the UFO."

Mike also said, "This contract that we have is seriously behind schedule. In fact, Monday the time is up. We haven't done any work on it since Wednesday because of this thing; therefore, it won't be done. I hope they take that into account, this problem. As it is, we have to drive an hour and fifteen minutes one way, both to and from work. It's hard for us to get in a regular eight-hour day. It usually ends up being around six or seven hours."

So, if a hoax was involved, Mike's candid admission of contract difficulties could be construed as a motive. But Mike also said, "If it hadn't been for the fact that Walton was missing, I don't think that we'd have said anything to anybody but our families about [seeing] it. We never would have reported it."

He seemed genuinely concerned about the fate of the missing man.

"The thing that aggravates me about this," he said, "is that I made mention of using a helicopter, horses, and that maybe we could use bloodhounds. I mentioned this to several different officers, and it was just like it went in one ear and out the other. Nobody seemed that interested in searching that extensively. No bloodhounds were brought in. And now it's too late. I've been mentioning it every day."

He didn't want to fault Sheriff Gillespie, who at least was personally conducting the investigation. Gillespie had recounted several stories of his experiences with UFOs.

He had told the stories to fellow police officers long before Walton disappeared, and he retold them during the search.

"He's the only one who believes the six men's story," Duane said. "Everybody else has been treating it with a whole lot of ridicule, sniggering behind their hands and laughing up their sleeves."

"Chuck Ellison kind of treats it fair," Mike said. "I don't like to say that they did anything really wrong. I just say that they should have, right off the bat, done a much more extensive search—assuming, of course, that he is still here to be found."

If he was, then he had been out in the woods for seventy-two hours, with just a light jacket to protect himself against plunging nighttime temperatures and no food.

The prospects of those conditions stimulated another furious outburst from Duane. "I don't believe he's hurt or injured in any way, and he'll be back sooner or later —whenever they get done doing what they're doing. I don't feel any fear for him at all. I only regret that I'm not able to experience the same thing. He's not missing. He knows where he's at, and I know where he's at. Basically . . ."

"He's not on the earth," Mike interjected.

"He's not in the woods." Duane rushed forward. "They took him for whatever purpose they take people—to run a few tests, probe his mind. . . ."

"Where do you feel he is?" Sylvanus asked.

"Not on this earth," Duane answered.

"You don't think he's on this earth?"

"Sure don't. It's ridiculous for man to assume that he's the only one civilized, technological society in a universe that's bigger than the average man in the street can begin to comprehend. It's ridiculous! The people aren't here to make war, or they'd have destroyed us a long time ago."

"Have either one of you fellows read much about flying saucers?" Sylvanus asked.

"A little," Mike answered.

"How about you, Duane?"

"As much as anybody."

"Well, some people have read a lot, and some have read a little."

"I'm not a fan," Mike said, "or, I wasn't until now."

"I follow it about like I do a lot of things," Duane said. "It's there. I know it's real. It's not a phenomenon to me. It's just one of those things."

For someone who had been accused of taking his brother's bizarre disappearance much too calmly, Duane was now emotionally all hyped up, rushing along irrepressibly, running his words and sentences all together in a swift flow of excitement.

"I've lived with it for the past ten or twelve years, I've been seeing them all the time, it's not new to me, it's not a surprise, it's not unique. . . ."

"You just feel it in your bones that he's going to come back," Sylvanus said.

"Sure do. It's just a matter of time. They don't kill people."

"Well, the funny part of it is," Sylvanus replied, "there have been too many incidents of them not coming back."

"If he doesn't come back," Duane retorted, "I don't believe that they're gonna kill him. They don't kill people. I mean, they would have killed him and left him lying there, or they'd kill him and . . ."

"You feel that he'll be found."

It was Duane's turn now to be irritated with Sylvanus.

"Yeah," he answered. "He'll either be found, or, if he doesn't come back, it'll be a voluntary thing, because he wanted to stay. It's also . . . it's also rather narrowminded to assume that this is the best place in the universe to be. There might be a better place. I'm not saying there is. I'm not saying I'd stay there if there was. But there is certainly a possibility."

The interview returned again to complaints about the search. Fifty men for five and a half hours was not nearly enough, Mike said.

"They needed one hundred fifty men for forty-eight hours," Duane said and fairly bristled.

"We've been accused of murdering him and stashing him somewhere and using the story to cover it up with," Mike noted.

Duane hotly responded, "Six men with such a variance in their backgrounds don't commit murder and then cover for one another. It's stupid, especially when all six of them are hollering for a lie detector—two lie detectors and two operators. . . . They want the sodium pentothal [truth serum], a hypnotist . . . and what have they got? A bunch of crap from the law enforcement agency!"

Sylvanus asked if he could be present for the lie-detector tests.

"I don't object if there are a lot of people there," Mike answered. "I'd like somebody there who knows a little bit about the lie-detector test so they can't cover up the results."

The thing about the search, Duane persisted, seemingly growing more angry every time he thought about it, was, "They started at ten in the morning, and they searched until two-thirty in the afternoon. They had something to check the radiation count on the ground, and that's all. They didn't have any horses, they didn't have any helicopters, and they didn't have any dogs. They brought lunch out around one o'clock, the guys ate, they kicked around in the bushes for another hour and a half or so, and then everybody pulled out. They were all gone, except the sheriff and his deputies. They stayed until dark, but they didn't stay in the immediate area.

"The next day, Friday, Mike and I stayed out there with my half brother until about nine-thirty or ten that night. . . . The next day, nobody, no one came out at all. . . Saturday, the sheriff's department made no contact with my mother or any other member of our family. They mentioned nothing to any of the men [Mike Rogers' crew]. . . . Well, maybe the polygraph man is coming today, maybe he's coming tomorrow . . . they're gonna give the tests, so just don't leave town.

"It's been almost seventy-two hours since the disappearance. Mike and I drove over to Holbrook and talked to Marlin Gillespie, who is concerned and who does believe the story. And we told him that we didn't think enough was being done, or didn't think enough had been done, and that everybody should get off their butts and get back to work. And that's why everybody was out here this evening. . . . They're gonna have more men back out here tomorrow, but only because Mike and I went over and raised a little hell with the sheriff's department."

"Would bloodhounds do any good now?" Sylvanus asked.

"It's froze, and I'm froze, and the wind's been blowing, and there's not a chance in the world," Duane answered.

"If they'd have got those dogs out here the first day or that next morning," Mike said, "it might have helped, but not now, especially after you've had hundreds of people walking around out here. The bloodhounds should have been the first thing they had out here. . . . They could have followed right to where he's at, if he's out there."

"He's not out there," Duane said almost in a whisper.

"I don't think he's out there now, either," Mike agreed.

"Certainly," Duane said, "the search should have been thorough enough to erase this question that he might be . . . lying in the bushes, in the skeptics' minds."

"Now, if they'd brought the bloodhounds out," Mike said, "and they'd done a search, they'd either have found him, if he's out here, or the bloodhounds wouldn't have found his scent anywhere, except where he walked from the truck to over there, if they took him. But as it is now, we can conclude more or less from the fact that we haven't been able to find him that he's probably not here anymore. But, still, that's not conclusive, because there was not a thorough enough search."

"Well," Duane said, "I don't feel any fear for his life. He's not in any danger. He'll turn up sooner or later, whenever they are ready, or whenever he's ready. He's having the experience of a lifetime. I don't think he's in any danger at all, and he'll turn up. About all I can say is that I wish I was with him."

Sylvanus wanted to know what Duane's optimism and analysis were based on.

"Everybody in my family . . ."

Then Mike interrupted. "Long-term consideration of the idea."

"We've paid a lot of attention to it," Duane said, taking over. "We've lived with it for ten years. The fact that they're here and we see them quite regularly and that they don't kill people—that's not why they're here. With the technological advances that they have and the sophisticated weaponry they must be capable of, if they wanted to kill anybody, they could annihilate the whole entire population, if that's what's on their mind. They're not here to make war.

"I refuse to put the beings or the craft, or whatever you want to call it, in the role of villains. They're not the villains. There's no good or bad here, as good and bad is good and bad. It's just that he's gone, and he's having the experience of a lifetime, and all I wish was that I was there."

He would wish it even more in the next few days—but not because of growing yearnings to join his brother in the experience of a lifetime.

4.

SNOWFLAKE WAS BESIEGED BY NEWS REPORTERS AND UFologists from across the nation and around the world, all impelled by sketchy stories of a back-country woodcutter abducted by a UFO "in full view of six horrified co-workers."

Though there had been a few previous "abduction" cases reported to the general public, none had ever been verified by independent witnesses. And none of the previously purported abductions had ever lasted more than a few hours.

Something very serious seemed to have happened in the northern Arizona woods, something of possible universal and historical impact.

It was dutifully reported that Sheriff Gillespie had not ruled out the possibility of foul play being responsible for Travis Walton's bizarre disappearance. But the sheriff also candidly admitted that he was somewhat stumped. He didn't know what to believe.

All the witnesses had remained consistent in their accounts of what had happened. Each had been asked to draw a picture of what he had seen, and all the pictures matched. The sheriff's investigation had led him to a strong conviction that neither drugs nor alcohol had played any role at all in the baffling case.

The "experts" seemed to think that a valid UFO encounter had occurred. Field Investigator Ray Jordan, representing the Aerial Phenomena Research Organization (APRO) and the National Investigations Committee on Aerial Phenomena (NICAP), reported that the available evidence supported the witnesses' story. "I haven't found anything in their stories to indicate a hoax," he said. The young men I've interviewed so far are all visibly shaken by the experience. I'm inclined to believe that they're telling the truth."

Field Investigator Bill Spaulding represented his own Ground Saucer Watch of Phoenix, the internationally prestigious Center for UFO Studies at Northwestern University, and the Mutual UFO Network (MUFON). He reported: "We found some interesting things up there [at the site]. If this is a hoax, it's one of the best I've ever seen." He also was inclined to believe the story.

Using Anis TM Gauss meters on the ground, slash piles, and surrounding trees, Spaulding claimed to have discovered high traces of residual magnetism—a circumstance consistent with the professional theory that extraterrestrial space vehicles were powered by anti-gravity engines. Spaulding's charts showed $+8$ Gauss at the woodpile over which the UFO allegedly hovered, and $+10$ to $+12$ Gauss in the area directly behind that. Normal ground and tree readings ranged from $+1$ to -2.

But on the side of the clearing opposite where the UFO had allegedly appeared, Spaulding claimed to have recorded a whopping -15 Gauss, suggesting a strong polarity reversal, possibly caused by anti-gravity power.

Spaulding noted that he had also discovered residual traces of ozone in the area.

Spaulding introduced himself to the Walton family at the search site, and he offered his future services, should the need arise. He was sure, he said, that Travis would need special help if he was returned, and he asked that Duane save Travis' clothing and his first urination after returning.

Meanwhile, Snowflake Town Marshal Sanford (Sank) Flake publicly announced his opinion: "One of these days," Sank said, "Travis is going to come walking in here with a wild story about taking a ride in a flying saucer. . . . I think the whole thing is a hoax, staged by Travis and his brother Duane to make some money. I believe the other kids did see something, but they were hoaxed, too. What they saw was an inflated rubber raft, or balloon, or something like that, all lit up electronically and hung in the trees to look like a UFO. Travis set them up, telling them stories about UFOs, and when he had them ready, it happened. They saw something rise up in the trees, all lighted up and made to look like a UFO. They didn't see him go on any UFO. They drove out of sight, scared to death it was gonna get them. They did exactly what they were supposed to do."

Sank Flake's schoolteacher wife bluntly told him, "Your idea is just as farfetched as Duane Walton's."

Duane Walton said, "Sank Flake is a typical, redneck, hick sheriff. He is just plain dumb."

Duane charged that Sank Flake was prejudiced because the Waltons were not descended from original settlers.

The Waltons were newcomers, having resided in Snowflake for only eight years—just a speck in time compared with families whose roots went back for generations. Some families had been on the same land for nearly a century. The Waltons were "different." They were high-spirited, and they had had some scrapes with fellow townsmen.

The outspoken Duane was considered an oddball, a kook, by the town's frontier standards of conservatism.

But it was Travis who was most often in the town's eye. He had been a wild teen-ager, and he had locked horns with the town marshal more than once. And more than once, Travis had won.

Sank Flake, a grandson of the town's co-founder, was a big, husky, sleepy-eyed, drawling Wyatt Earp, with a handlebar moustache. Though articulate, he was a plodding kind of thinker, not quickly perceptive and incisive like his brother Glen.

Whereas Glen was an open and generally outgoing man, Sank tended to be more cautious with people, more reserved, suspicious even, and not necessarily always judicious in his judgments.

Once, he jailed the then sixteen-year-old Travis for speeding. Sank did not witness the alleged infraction himself. Somebody else told him about it. So the next day he arrested Travis and locked him up in the town jail.

The previous occupant had been a "drunken Indian" who had vomited and defecated all over the floor and bed. Travis promptly escaped through the ceiling. He ran home and told his mother that he had fled because the smell and slime were making him sick. She packed him off to Holbrook to turn himself in to the sheriff.

Shortly thereafter, she claimed, Sank Flake "barged into" her home, looking for Travis. She read him the riot act: Sank had jailed a juvenile, did not read him his rights, did not file a specific charge, did not notify the juvenile's parent, and then tried to search her house without a warrant and without her permission. The "case" ended right there.

In later years, Sank made a conscious effort to downplay Travis' juvenile conduct: "just kid stuff, prankish, minor . . . it didn't amount to anything . . . just stuff that all kids get into. You know, some of them [in Travis' group] are these kids that fell into hippie ways, dirty all the time, with long hair tied back in kerchiefs, using drugs. . . . I'm not saying I ever caught him with any drugs; I didn't. But there were drugs being used. A lot of things happen that I can't prove."

Sank considered Travis a hippie, a rebel, not the kind of kid he was used to, not one he liked very much.

And in 1971, Travis and Mike Rogers' brother, Charles, did get caught stealing and forging payroll checks from Snowflake's Western Molding Company. Charles Rogers worked there; Travis had worked there part-time. They stole blank checks, made them out to fictitious people, signed the forged signature of company president Robert Gonsalves, and cashed them. On May 5, 1971, they pleaded guilty to first-degree burglary and forgery charges brought in Navajo County Superior Court. They made complete restitution, served two years of satisfactory probation, and were permitted to retract their original guilty pleas so that their records could be expunged under provisions of Arizona law.

A teacher at the high school had told Sank Flake that Travis had tested out to genius on IQ tests, and he could well believe it. Travis was a smart cookie. In succeeding years, townsmen generally viewed Travis without great affection. However, they considered him grown up from his wayward juvenile days.

To some degree, the townspeople agreed with Duane Walton's harsh assessment of Marshal Flake: "He's just plain dumb."

Meanwhile, Sank was conducting his own search for

the missing man. He searched the Bear Springs ranch several times, sure that was where Travis was hiding. He even took a London television crew out with him once, possibly to film his capture live.

But he never found a trace of Travis there or anyplace else.

He told Mary Walton Kellet and Duane that he didn't believe the UFO story at all, because he never saw UFOs. And he claimed that they replied rather hotly: " 'Why don't you look up? Maybe you'll see something if only you look up. Or maybe you need a special intelligence to be in tune with *them*.' She told me she saw them all the time out there at the ranch. One evening, she said, she just sat out there on the porch and watched them swooping in and out. A dozen or more of them were just flying around there. She told me about watching this whole fleet of them just flying in and out of that ranch. . . . The family talked about it all the time. Duane even said that he and Travis had made a pact that they would contact each other if either one of them was ever taken."

Sank, however, had not been precisely truthful when he told Mary and Duane that he didn't believe the UFO story because he had never seen one. In fact, he had seen one—what he thought was a UFO—and it had chased him home in a terrible fright years before. The experience was not one that Sank revealed until much later.

His brother Glen did not totally agree with Sank's hoax theory. But he was having some doubts. The press reported that Travis, Duane, and their mother were "outspoken believers in UFOs" prior to the disappearance. Duane was quoted as saying that he and his brother had seen over a dozen UFOs in as many years, and "five or six were just as definite as anything you could imagine." In various press versions, Mary had previously expressed interest in being abducted, or Duane had, or Travis, or all three. The unsubstantiated rumors of the family's alleged long-standing obsession with UFOs were widely reprinted as if they were all corroborated facts. These rumors had a strong effect on the ensuing controversy.

Glen didn't know how much of the rumormongering was true, but Mary had told him that a UFO had chased one of them, or all of them——he wasn't sure. Then, during the search, Mike and Kenny had said how funny it was ——"We were just talking about that, talking about UFOs coming home after work in the truck." Glen's impression was that they were always talking about it. And then, suddenly, it happened to them. That just seemed peculiar to Glen Flake, especially since it was the Waltons who were so deeply involved.

The Waltons, meanwhile, were being hounded by reporters and policemen alike. The reporters wanted endless interviews, and Duane, especially, was most obliging. But his anger soon surfaced over the manner in which some newspapers and television news shows were reporting the story. Rumors, gossip, innuendo, occasional outright slander, and defamation of character caused Duane's already short fuse to light up, and he exploded in several furious tirades. He was particularly incensed at so-called UFO "experts" who were quoted as saying that "abductions" never lasted this long, or, if they did, then the "abductees" were never returned.

With some justification, Duane pointed out that his mother was being brutally victimized by all the loose reportorial talk. After all, that was her son everybody was talking about. On the one hand, that son was being accused, in absentia, of perpetrating a hoax, maybe. On the other, maybe he was snatched by spacemen from another world, and if he wasn't returned by now, perhaps he never would be.

"That," said Duane, "sure doesn't help my mother any. She is suffering enough as it is."

However, her reaction itself had become a matter of public speculation, mainly because several deputies had opined out loud that she hadn't seemed too concerned about her son's disappearance. So was she really suffering?

Her closest neighbors thought she was, even those who did not believe the UFO story. They saw her every day, and she was strained, tense, and her whole face was tightened up with anxiety and suppressed fear.

Mrs. Glen Flake didn't believe the UFO story, but she certainly was not in agreement with the things that people were saying about Travis Walton's mother——that she was in on the hoax, that she was hiding him, that she was acting suspiciously, saying suspicious things, and was not at all worried.

Mrs. Flake told her family, "I know she was not in on it, whatever is going on. She is suffering, really and truly. I saw her in the store, and I know. She is worried to death. But she is trying to hold it all inside of herself. When I saw her, I never felt so sorry for anybody in my life. She looks like she has aged ten years just in the past few days. Her eyes are just shot full with her pain."

Several deputies intent on cracking the case, spent hours on end camped out in Mary's living room, grilling her incessantly, asking the same unanswerable questions that had already been asked dozens of times before.

One evening, Duane walked in on one such interrogation. He had been up to the sheriff's office in Holbrook with the six witnesses. When he entered the house, a deputy was sitting there questioning his mother. She was very upset, and she was crying. But the deputy just sat there, talking and talking and talking at her while she wept. It was one of the few times that Duane had ever seen his mother cry in front of anyone else.

Very steely and precise, Duane told the deputy, "Let's you and I go outside and talk."

The deputy followed Duane out to the front porch, and Duane told him not to come back unless he had something concrete on his mind. There would be no more fishing expeditions at his mother's expense.

When he returned to the house, Duane said, "Mother, from here on out, when any of these jokers comes around and wants to come in and just keep hashing this thing over and over, don't you do it. Don't let them in. You go out on the porch and talk to them. Then, if you become upset, you can come back inside and shut the door. You have your privacy. This is your home. That man was sitting there, and he could see you were in tears, and he didn't have enough thoughtfulness about him to excuse himself and beg your forgiveness and get out. He was just sitting there prodding your wounds. You talk to them on the front porch. Then you can retire when you're ready. You don't have to get rude and tell them to leave. You can leave when you want."

The next morning, Marshal Sank Flake knocked on her front door. She did not have a telephone, and the police were carrying messages back and forth to the house all the time. She opened the door, came out on the porch, and closed the door behind her. Flake was a little surprised at her action, because normally she would have invited him inside, even though he had had some bitter confrontations with the family in the past. And he had also made some blunt statements about this latest escapade, had flat-out told the press what he thought about the UFO tale—it was a hoax, to his way of thinking.

Now, suddenly, Mary did not seem to want him coming into the house. He kind of wondered about that. But he just gave her the message and left.

That was Monday morning, November 10, the fifth day of Travis Walton's disappearance. It was the day on which Sheriff Gillespie was finally going to resolve the nagging question of whether or not Travis had been murdered, buried, and the entire UFO story concocted by the rest of the crew to conceal the foul deed.

The investigation had revealed that there had been bad blood between some of the men. Travis and Allen Dalis especially did not get along. Both were volatile personalities—egotistic, opinionated, hot-tempered, aggressive.

Also, even though they had been close friends for about seven years, Travis and Mike Rogers often argued fiercely, though usually the arguments were no more than heated debates, intellectual battles. They both had good minds, inquisitive natures, and they were both as outspoken as they were well spoken.

Even so, the sheriff mused, it wouldn't have been the first time that a purely intellectual battle had gotten out of hand, with mayhem resulting. Fights always had to start somewhere. The sheriff knew from experience that hot words were as quick a trigger as anything.

But the baffled sheriff also recognized that a conspiracy of either hoax or murder seemed unlikely for this mixed-bag crew. Mike Rogers and Kenny Peterson were both reputed to be straight arrows, utterly decent and trustworthy. Steve Pierce was still a boy and not personally close to anybody in the crew. Dwayne Smith was from Phoenix and had been on the job for only three days, hardly enough time to get thick with a pack of deliberately scheming conspirators, whether hoaxers or murderers.

This just was not a close, unified, tightly knit group, by any means. And the sheriff's interrogations had not dislodged even a single discrepancy from the group's common and consistent story.

Sheriff Gillespie felt that he was duty-bound to explore every possibility, make use of every available investigative tool. One such tool was the polygraph, less accurately known as the lie detector.

So on Monday morning Sheriff Gillespie summoned Mike Rogers and his crew of wood-cutters to Holbrook. Awaiting them at the sheriff's headquarters was Cy Gilson, polygraph examiner of the Arizona Department of Public Safety, who had traveled up from Phoenix to assist in the investigation.

Gilson was asked primarily to determine if a crime had been committed. The crux of it was: Had any violence been done to Travis Walton? But Sheriff Gillespie also requested that the men be questioned about the UFO, because he also wanted to determine if the story was a hoax—if "the whole damned bunch of them is involved in a hoax."

The men arrived at about ten o'clock, and they were briefed on what was happening. All agreed to participate in the testing. Each man was given four tests, lasting about twenty minutes each. Much of the time was spent sitting around a small kitchen, waiting to be strapped to the polygraph machine. It was boring. Several of the guys went outside to shoot baskets at a backyard court, but the reporters and camermen mobbed them, driving them back inside. It was weird, they agreed, how everybody was acting. Crazy. Insane. And they think we're nuts!

The testing lasted until ten o'clock that night.

The final results depended on Gilson's four relevant questions:

1). *Did you cause Travis Walton any serious physical injury last Wednesday afternoon?*

2). *Do you know if Travis Walton was physically injured by some other member of your work crew last Wednesday?*

3). *Do you know if Travis Walton's body is buried or hidden somewhere in the Turkey Springs area?*

4). *Did you tell the truth about actually seeing a UFO last Wednesday when Travis Walton disappeared? (One variation added to this basic question was: Do you believe that Travis Walton was actually taken aboard a UFO last Wednesday?)*

There were no deceptive responses to any of the questions asked of five of the six men. The sixth man was Allen Dalis. Gilson was puzzled, even bewildered a little, by Dalis. While all the other men cooperated fully, Dalis, in Gilson's opinion, behaved completely the opposite. He wouldn't cooperate; he was belligerent. Gilson couldn't make heads or tails of any of his tests. Dalis was not necessarily lying, Gilson told the sheriff; his tests were definitely inconclusive.

"I have no idea what he is all about," Gilson said. "But there is no question about the other men. They are telling the truth. They haven't done anything to Travis Walton. They don't know anything about anyone else doing anything to him. And they are telling the truth about actually seeing a UFO on the night he disappeared, which doesn't prove that they actually saw one; they may have. But the test only determined that they truthfully believe that they saw one. There is just no way that this many people can get together and devise a system to beat the machine. There are too many involuntary responses involved, physical and emotional responses that cannot be controlled at will. Some people can, but they are rare. The odds would be astronomical against this many people, acquainted with each other, all living and working in the same place, and all of them possessing that rare control required to beat the machine."

"There is no doubt?" Gillespie asked.

"There is none."

Gilson's official report stated:

Each of the six men answered "No" to questions #1, 2, and 3, and they each answered "Yes" to question #4. The test results were conclusive on Goulette, Smith, Peterson, Rogers, and Pierce. The test results on Dalis were inconclusive.

Based on the polygraph chart tracing, it is the opinion of this examiner that Goulette, Smith, Peterson, Rogers, and Pierce were being truthful when they answered these relevant questions.

These polygraph examinations prove that these five men did see some object that they believe to be a UFO, and that Travis Walton was not injured or murdered by any of these men on that Wednesday [November 5, 1975]. If an actual UFO did not exist and the UFO is a man-made hoax, five of these men had no prior knowledge of a hoax. No such determination can be made of the sixth man, whose test results were inconclusive.

Sheriff Gillespie was not especially bothered by the singled flawed test. He announced, "There's no doubt they're telling the truth—right down the line. I thought at first there was a very good possibility it was a hoax, but not now. I've been in law enforcement for over eighteen years, and I've never known anything like this. I feel sure that all six of them saw a UFO."

Still, why didn't Dalis test out conclusively like the others?

Mike Rogers offered some insight into Dalis: "Allen is a coward, kind of. He's also kind of a hoodlum. You might call him the black sheep of the crew."

To which Marshal Sank Flake added: "Dalis is the only one of that bunch that I had any real trouble with in town. He's got sticky fingers. I know he pulled a couple of burglaries that I couldn't pin on him. I wouldn't trust him as far as I could throw him. Since he's the only one who didn't 'pass' the lie test, I'd almost have to believe the opposite with him. Not 'passing' means he's probably telling the truth. He saw it, the UFO."

In addition, Dalis was an occasional drug user, and probably most fearful of being asked something about the darker aspects of his secretive life. And he had no great fondness for authority to begin with.

His hostile and uncooperative attitude may have erupted from all of these factors. Or his resistance may have been rooted in some other source. But no one was very much disturbed that Dalis had not passed the polygraph test.

The convincing manner in which the other five witnesses passed their tests was far too impressive to be anything but overwhelming. Though the polygraph could not prove that Travis had been abducted by a UFO, it seemed to prove that the witnesses' whole story could very well be true. Their story was that Travis apparently had been picked up by a UFO.

And that made some of the original disbelievers a little nervous. It was just a little bit scary to acknowledge that a UFO might swoop down at any minute and snatch up somebody else, though nobody really panicked at the prospect. Even so, a few folks did elect to stay indoors at night, and they made sure that all their doors were locked.

Mary Walton Kellet was not greatly relieved by the test results because she had never believed that the boys had done any harm to Travis in the first place. Now she just hoped that with the fruitless search in the woods, and the polygraph tests . . . maybe that would settle all the wild stories that were circulating. Maybe people would stop accusing and start thinking.

But her son was still missing, so she kept praying, the only solution she knew of. She believed in prayer. A Mormon convert, she was not fanatical. She drank coffee and smoked cigarettes, both scorned by strict Mormons. But when you've got a problem, she figured, and there doesn't seem to be any way that you can solve it, then you ask God to help you. She believed the story that Mike had told her, she believed every word of it, had no reason to question it—even that Travis seemed to have gone off on the UFO. She believed every word of it. All she knew to do about it was to keep trusting in God that Travis would be all right.

The sardonic comment of one neighbor, John Ballard, was hardly comforting: "If *they* were looking for a perfect human specimen," he said, "they'll bring him back pretty soon. Don't you worry about that."

5.

AT ABOUT MIDNIGHT THE TELEPHONE RANG AT TRAVIS' sister's home in Taylor. Allison's husband, Grant Neff, answered.

"This is Travis," a very strained voice said. "I'm in a phone booth at the Heber gas station, and I need help. Come and get me."

The voice seemed to gasp. It sounded strangely confused, distant, and tremulous. To Grant, it did not sound like his missing brother-in-law. Instead, he thought it was just another of the hoax calls that they'd been getting all week.

"I'm sorry," Grant said, "but you must have the wrong number."

"Oh, no, I haven't!" the voice screamed at him. "It's me, Grant. Don't you hang up on me. It's Travis. I'm hurt and I need help badly. You come and get me."

The voice was knifed with genuine hysteria.

"All right," Grant replied, shaken himself. "You hang on. I'll get your brother and we'll be right there."

He hurriedly told his wife what had happened, then left the house and drove swiftly over to his mother-in-law's in Snowflake, three miles away.

Duane had been up to Holbrook for the polygraph tests. On his return, he had picked up his mother at the Neffs' and took her home. They had just been home a little while, sitting there talking, when Grant came in the front door. His face was as white as a sheet.

"I just got a call," he said, "from Travis."

And he recounted the telephone conversation.

Duane jumped up and said, "Let's go!"

"Mary, if you will," Grant said, "go stay with Allison and the babies until we get back."

It took Duane and Grant less than thirty minutes to drive the thirty miles to Heber. They found Travis crumpled up on the floor of the second phone booth at the gas station. He was conscious, but he seemed to be suffering from some kind of shock. The temperature was about eighteen degrees, and he was shivering, clothed only in a cotton shirt, Levi's, and a Levi jacket.

They got him out of the phone booth and into the car, and they immediately sped back toward Snowflake. Travis seemed wrought up, in a turmoil, and only vaguely described where he had been and what had happened to him.

Apparently, he had been on a spacecraft with creatures whose terrific eyes still burned in his memory. He couldn't get the eyes out of his head. He was frightened, and he was not communicating too well.

"Everybody has been worried sick about you," Duane told him.

Travis seemed surprised. "It's only been a couple of hours," he said. "What time is it now?"

He seemed to believe that it was still Wednesday, November 5, the day he had disappeared.

"Travis," Duane said, "feel your face."

He did. His face was rough with a thick growth of beard.

"You've been gone five days," Duane said.

For a moment, Travis seemed not to understand. His eyes frowned. And then he shook his head, and he mumbled in disbelief, bewildered, very upset, and he slouched down defensively, not wanting to talk anymore about it.

When they arrived at his mother's house, Duane got Travis undressed and into a bathtub full of warm water. He was very thirsty, very hungry, and very tired. Duane fed him sips of water and chips of ice, and then he gave him some cottage cheese and pecan cookies. The food made him sick to his stomach, but he couldn't get enough water.

At six-feet-two, he had a slender, sinewy build, but it was still obvious that he had lost some weight. Duane put him on the bathroom scale, and he weighed one hundred fifty-four pounds, about eleven pounds under his normal weight.

"Well, I'm gonna get him out of this small town," Duane decided. "He's in no condition to be interrogated by the police and the reporters and everybody else. We've had enough of that harassment already. I'm gonna get him out of here, and down to Phoenix, where he can get some help."

Grant drove back to his own home, where Mary and Allison were waiting.

"Well, it's really him," he said. "He's home now, and he looks in pretty bad shape. If you want to see him, Allison, you go see him, because Duane's going to take him to Phoenix."

When Mary saw him, she knew he was not normal. His mind seemed jumbled, confused, and disoriented, very unlike him. Normally, his mind was quick, sharp. He was never at a loss for words. But now his tongue stumbled a bit, and he seemed withdrawn. He didn't want to talk, period.

Her impression was that he wanted a doctor, and he didn't want the police to know he was there. He seemed to be repeating it, like some litany he had learned or memorized: "Don't let the police know I'm here. . . . I've got to have a doctor. . . . Don't let the police know. . . . Get me some medical help. . . ." In his condition, she couldn't understand where he was getting that from. But he was adamant: no police; he needed a doctor.

At two-thirty that morning, Sheriff Gillespie received a tip from somebody at the telephone company that the call had been made from one of the Heber booths. There were three booths in a row at the gas station on Highway 260, the main route south toward Phoenix.

Gillespie ordered Lieutenant E. M. Romo to get down to Heber, pick up Deputy Chuck Ellison, and dust all the phones for Travis Walton's fingerprints. The sheriff wanted to positively identify Travis as the one who made the call to Grant Neff. He had no intention of getting unhinged by a fake call now. After telling Romo to also check around Heber for any Walton family cars, he called Deputy Glen Flake in Snowflake and ordered him to drive out to the fork on Route 277 and watch for one of the Walton or Neff cars. The left fork in the road went to

Snowflake, where the Waltons lived, and the right went to Taylor, where the Neffs lived.

It was three A.M. when Romo and Ellison started dusting the phones in the freezing cold. Two were covered with prints, but none they could identify as belonging to Travis Walton. The third phone was wiped completely clean of all fingerprints. It was one of the end booths. The sheriff's men couldn't understand why it was wiped clean. One possible reason, they speculated, was that maybe no one had used the phone since the serviceman had last collected the money from the coin boxes. The collector always wiped the phones clean after emptying the coin boxes.

It was nearly six o'clock in the morning when the deputies finished. They had been working in less than ideal conditions, in the cold and dark, and maybe they had just flat missed Travis' prints—or maybe the prints had never been there in the first place.

They had also made a search of Heber's streets, but they found no Walton or Neff cars. They advised the sheriff of all this.

Meanwhile, Glen Flake had watched the Heber fork, and no cars at all came through—not the family's, not anyone's. The sheriff told him to take a ride over to the mother's house and see if anything was going on.

When he got there, the lights were on and there seemed to be some sort of hubbub inside the house. There was a truck and trailer parked outside, and Duane was siphoning gas from it. The truck belonged to a family friend. Duane had driven back from Holbrook too late to fill his own gas tank. The stations were all closed at that time of night.

So he simply told Glen Flake, "Yes, I'm a working man, too, you know. I've got to run on down to Phoenix, but I should be back again tomorrow, I imagine."

Nothing else was said. Flake did not ask about the phone call, he didn't ask about Travis, and he didn't ask to go inside. And Duane did not tell him that Travis had returned.

Flake drove away. Shortly thereafter, Duane bundled Travis into his car and headed for his home in Glendale, on the west side of Phoenix. According to Duane, both the press and the police had already hounded the family unmercifully. And Travis—frightened, confused, almost mute—just wasn't ready for that yet. He wanted a doctor, and he didn't want to talk to anyone about what had happened to him.

In a strict technical sense, Travis was a fugitive of sorts, in flight from the police, because some days before Sheriff Gillespie had issued an All Points Bulletin for him. But it was the family's contention that first things came first. And the main thing to them was to protect Travis from what they had been undergoing during his disappearance. Duane also said that with Travis in Phoenix, Mary would be spared the clamor and tumult that were sure to engulf him once the press and police learned that he had returned.

The two brothers arrived at Duane's home early Tuesday morning. Following the advice of Ground Saucer Watch Director Bill Spaulding, Duane allegedly preserved Travis' first urination after returning, plus the clothes he had worn during his absence. At the search site, Spaulding had said that both would be invaluable for testing purposes. "If your brother should ever return," Duane recalled Spaulding saying, "we can offer all the scientific testing he'll need. Just call me, and I'll arrange everything."

Duane called him. Travis was back and he needed medical help, a complete physical examination by a good doctor. Spaulding told him to go to Dr. Lester Steward, GSW's medical consultant, whose office was in the Westward-Ho Motel.

It was nine-thirty when Travis and Duane arrived there. To Travis, the place looked rundown and seedy, not at all the first-rate motel it had been in years past. They found Dr. Steward's room number on the lobby directory and took the elevator up.

The sign on the door read: DR. STEWARD—HYPNOTHERAPIST.

"Spaulding told me he was a medical doctor," Duane said, suspicious.

Nonetheless, they went in and introduced themselves to Steward. He said he had been expecting them. Duane explained what they were seeking—a complete medical examination.

"Are you a medical doctor?"

"Yes," Steward answered, "but I don't have immediate access to medical or laboratory facilities required to do tests such as are needed here."

He briefly questioned Travis about his experience, and Travis replied succinctly, volunteering few details.

Travis did not like the air of either Steward or his office—unsavory, unhealthy, he thought. There were no professional volumes in the room, the curtains were yellowed, and there was no air conditioning. The windows were open and the room was racketed by the roar of jet planes screaming overhead. He asked for a drink of water, and the glass Steward gave him was dirty, smudged up by the lips and fingers of previous users. He was disgusted and mentally labeled the place the Westward Ho-Ho Motel.

Duane, pressing for Steward's medical qualifications, finally got the doctor to admit that he was not licensed to practice in the state of Arizona.

"Well, we're just going to have to have a doctor," Duane said, "and that's all there is to it." He was getting angry.

"All right," Steward responded. "I'll try to get in touch with a doctor friend of mine on the telephone."

He made the call, and from what the brothers could overhear, Steward's doctor friend did not remember him. "It's me . . . Steward . . . Lester Steward . . . you remember. . . ."

This guy is a quack, Duane thought. And all of a sudden, he said, "Something's not right here. Let's blow."

They left, with Steward calling behind them that he was going to get a doctor if they would just wait.

They stopped for breakfast a few blocks away, the first real meal Travis had had since returning, and then they drove on to Duane's house, in Glendale. By then the telephone was ringing constantly. Someone had informed the news media that Travis was back. Outside the family, the only people who knew were Spaulding and Steward. Duane was determined to have nothing more to do with either one of them, and he so informed them when they both called, trying to reenter the case.

Meanwhile, Duane had devised a cover story to get the press and other callers off his back. They were told that Travis had been placed in a private Tucson hospital where he was undergoing a complete physical examination

—brain scan, urinalysis, blood testing, radiology, the full works. And neither Travis nor the test results would be available for several days.

The Aerial Phenomena Research Organization was based in Tucson. It was one of the more respected UFology investigative groups, adhering strictly to formal scientific methodology in its examination and judgment of claimed UFO experiences. Its representatives were located worldwide, based in over fifty countries. And its staff and consulting experts were composed almost exclusively of holders of advanced academic degrees, usually a Ph. D. or M.D.

The international director of the group was Jim Lorenzen. His wife, Coral, was secretary-treasurer. APRO investigators had been keeping them abreast of developments in the Travis Walton case, and when they were informed that Travis had reportedly been admitted to a Tucson hospital, the Lorenzens checked all the local hospitals, trying to find him.

Eventually, they decided that he must really be at his brother Duane's. So Coral called there and identified herself to Duane's wife, Carol, whereupon Duane took the phone.

"We've been trying to reach you for several minutes," Mrs. Lorenzen explained, "because we did get a call from someone else regarding Travis' return, and we think you probably need medical help for your brother."

"That's exactly right," Duane said. He described what had happened with Spaulding and Steward, who now appeared to be angry because they had been dropped from the case.

"Travis has told us that he needs a doctor," Duane said, "and they were supposed to get a doctor, but they just left us sitting there. Travis is still quite upset, he's scared, and he's suspicious of being hurt further."

"We will get you a doctor," Mrs. Lorenzen replied. "Just sit tight. Don't go anywhere. A doctor will be in touch with you."

Duane agreed to cooperate.

At noon, the *National Enquirer,* with its long-standing publishing interest in UFO cases, called APRO in Tucson. Coral Lorenzen was asked her opinion of the Walton story. From the evidence so far, she replied, it looked legitimate. "Right now, we don't see how a hoax could have been perpetrated, and we are convinced that something quite bizarre happened to him. Of course, a great many tests need to be conducted. Every detail of the story must be corroborated, if possible. We are going to provide such services as are available to us for the testing and so forth. But we don't have unlimited finances."

She told the *Enquirer* that Travis' physical and emotional state apparently were not yet stable enough to allow him to cope with his experience fully—certainly he could not withstand an onslaught from the press. And probably he should be rendered anonymous for the moment.

The *Enquirer* agreed to pay for a hotel room in which Travis and his brother could be sequestered. An *Enquirer* investigating team would be dispatched to Phoenix, and it would pick up the tab for other expenses incurred during the investigation.

At three-thirty that afternoon, two APRO doctors arrived at Duane's house to examine Travis. They were Dr. Howard Kandell, medical director of Health Maintenance Associates, and Dr. Joseph Saults.

Kandell's subsequent report described what was found:

Travis Walton, age twenty-two, was examined by me, along with Joseph Saults, M.D., on November 11, 1975, at approximately three-thirty P.M. The subject had disappeared the evening of November 5 and was subsequently found about midnight November 10, having allegedly been abducted by a UFO.

Travis was examined at his brother's [Duane Walton] home in Phoenix. We were asked by Duane at the time to confine our questions to those pertinent to his medical evaluation, since Travis was quite upset regarding this encounter.

Travis was lying in bed on his back, dressed in blue jeans, shirt, and socks. We were introduced to him by his brother. He was alert and oriented as to time, place, and person. He appeared anxious, though calm. He spoke slowly and showed no emotion at all, *i.e.*, his affect was extremely flat. He briefly related what he recalled occurred during the abduction, which was essentially the same information obtained during subsequent questioning. He specifically denied any physical contact with the beings he encountered, such as receiving any injections, intravenous injections, or infusions. He did not recall eating or drinking or going to the bathroom during his five-day disappearance. His weight on a bathroom scale in Heber [sic], Arizona, shortly after being found was one hundred fifty-four pounds, as reported by Duane.

He stripped to his undershorts for the examination.

Vital Signs: pulse, 76; respiration, 16; B.P. 110/68. He was well built, with no overt signs of weight loss [allegedly lost approximately ten pounds], though his mouth was somewhat dry. He had been eating and drinking fluids during the fifteen-hour interval since being found. He was basically clean [did not bathe or shower since found] and had no body odor, though he did have a three- to five-day growth of facial hair."

(Kandell was in error about Travis not having bathed.)

There were no bruises or evidence of trauma, except for a two-mm red spot in the crease of his right elbow, which was suggestive of a needle puncture; however, it was not overlying any significant blood vessel. He denied being aware of its presence and did not know what it might be due to.

The remainder of his examination was completely normal. His weight in my office two days later was one hundred sixty-three pounds dressed.

Duane, his brother, gave me a jar containing a urine specimen, which he said was Travis' first voiding subsequent to his being found.

The following laboratory studies were done on Travis Walton [under the alias of William Wilson, to avoid publicity at the time].

1). Urinalysis—volume, 560 cc: normal, with good concentration [SpG 1.032]; however, there was no acetone present, which is unusual, considering that any person who is without adequate nutrition for twenty-four to forty-eight hours will break down his own body-fat stores, which should result in ketones [acetones] being excreted into the urine. The absence of ketones in his urine, considering a ten-pound weight loss, is difficult to explain.

A drug screen run by the Maricopa County medical examiner's office, toxicology division, revealed no detectable drugs in that initial specimen submitted.

2). Chest X ray—normal.

3). EKG—normal.

4). EEG—normal.

5). Chemistries—SMA 12-normal.

In conclusion, the following points deserve further consideration:

1). His emotional state suggested that he had been through a disturbing experience.

2). Significance of his relatively clean state—if he had been lost in the woods for five to six days.

3). Significance of the *lack* of ketones in his first voided urine after being found, if, indeed, the ten-pound weight loss did occur.

4). Significance of possible puncture mark in elbow crease.

At the present time, one can only speculate as to the significance of the above.

Speculation would, indeed, be forthcoming. But Kandell himself thought that it was all very puzzling. Travis showed no signs of radiation exposure, his condition was not that of a man who had been wandering around in the woods for five days, and he appeared to be dehydrated, but apparently he had received some nourishment during his disappearance. The two-mm red spot, suggestive of a needle puncture, was "like the kind you get from a blood test," Kandell said. But Travis claimed no memory of being medically examined in any way while he was allegedly aboard the UFO. Rather, he said, the wound, several days old and healing, looked like a thorn wound normally suffered by the wood-cutters during their work.

"We work a lot on thorny brush out there," he said. "The chainsaw hits that buck brush and slaps it right back at you. It sticks those thorns right into you. I don't remember getting this one that way, but we always get them. and usually we don't even realize it."

The fundamental sum of the thorough medical examination was that there was nothing physically wrong with Travis Walton. And further testing of his blood and urine determined that there was no trace of drugs in his body.

Meanwhile, Sheriff Gillespie was trying to find Travis, and he was somewhat peeved at the run-around he was getting. All he knew was what he heard on news reports. The news reports said Travis was in a Tucson hospital. But no Tucson hospital had admitted Travis Walton, by his own or any other name. The sheriff wanted to know what was going on, and why he had been notified of the alleged victim's return only through the media. Why hadn't the family notified him directly, and immediately? His office had spent over ten thousand dollars searching for the missing man, several vehicles had been damaged in the rugged woods, one horse had been injured so badly that it had to be destroyed, and when the missing man eventually showed up again, the family spirited him out of town. What were they trying to hide? the sheriff wondered.

Duane finally telephoned Gillespie and explained that the family was only doing what it thought was best for Travis' protection. Travis was undergoing tests and treatment in a Tucson hospital, and the sheriff could interview him in the next few days.

But late Tuesday, Sheriff Gillespie learned that Travis was in Phoenix, after all. Bristling, he took off for Duane's house.

The press had also taken its toll on him. For nearly a week, the sheriff had not only personally conducted the investigation into the disappearance of Travis Walton, in addition to performing his more routine administrative duties, but he also personally handled most of the worldwide press queries about the alleged UFO abduction. He was constantly on the telephone, and as each phone interview ended, there was still another reporter waiting in person to be told the same story all over again. Quite patiently, the sheriff always responded, repeating the litany of events to date.

He was exhausted, and when he did get some sleep, it was a fitful respite. It was nearly midnight when the sheriff finally caught up with Travis Walton in his brother's Glendale home.

By then, only dribbles of his fantastic story had leaked

out, and much of that was distorted and erroneous. But, basically, the accounts claimed that Travis had been taken aboard an alien spaceship, had been examined in a hospital-like room by hairless and soundless dwarfs, and later woke up on the darkened highway outside Heber.

The sheriff's interrogation brought out a few more details. But the questioning was brief. Travis appeared to be suffering from distress, and the sheriff's anger cooled, subsiding in his compassionate nature.

Travis was lying down, unshaven, seemingly weak and distraught from his alleged horrific experience. He told the bare bones of his story in a frail monotone, apparently unwilling or unable to elaborate beyond sketchy details.

It was certainly a strange story, the sheriff mused. But was it true? He was especially interested in Travis' description of being hit by the beam of blue-green light allegedly fired into him from the UFO. Travis explained that he didn't actually remember seeing the beam itself. He saw the whole area suddenly light up brilliantly, and then he felt a tremendous shock that rendered him numb just before he passed out completely.

But he remembered the shock vividly. He described it as a terrific blow, as if he had been hit with a baseball bat. And he seemed to shudder just with the recollection of it.

The sheriff suggested that maybe Travis had been fooled, duped. Maybe he had been hit with some blunt instrument like a baseball bat. Maybe he had been assaulted, then drugged, and maybe he had actually awakened in a hospital examining room—perhaps drugs had distorted his perception of the experience. Theoretically, the sheriff thought, someone from the work crew could have walloped Travis, for whatever reason.

But no, Travis disagreed. There were no bumps on his head. No drugs had been detected in the tests made of his body chemistry. And just before he had been hit, he had turned to look back at the crew, yelling at him, and they were all sitting in Mike Rogers' truck, a hundred feet away from him. His story, he insisted, was true, just as he was telling it. And he was willing to take a lie-detector test to prove it.

To all this, Duane added, "A lie detector, truth serum, hypnosis, voice stress, or any other test you want to give him—he'll take them all."

The polygraph would do nicely, thank you, the sheriff replied. He would really be stumped if Travis passed the lie test, he thought. In fact, he admitted quite frankly, "I'm nearly stumped now."

Travis' account of what had happened in the woods fit exactly with the story told by the other witnesses. However, Travis' continuation of the tale left the sheriff unconvinced. He did not know if the story itself was at fault, or if his own ingrained attitudes made it difficult for him to believe that such events were really possible.

Publicly, he announced, "There were no contradictions in his story. And he denied emphatically that it was a hoax. But I personally have the feeling that the part about going into the UFO, the flying saucer . . . I have my doubts about that."

His under-sheriff, Deputy Ken Coplan, was less guarded in his reaction. "More than ever," he said, "I believe the story is a hoax. It's just too much to buy."

And just for good measure, famed psychic Peter Hurkos stamped his seal of disapproval on the case. "It's a hoax," he concluded long distance for the *Arizona Republic*. "I believe that there are unidentified flying objects. In fact, the government is aware of these. But this one is a hoax, someone's fantasy."

At no time in the following months was Travis Walton's story ever told completely and accurately, in print or on television. Most of the investigators, police, and UFologists alike were basing their reports and conclusions on that defective evidence—evidence that was incomplete, evidence that was further sullied by rumor, gossip, innuendo, and sometimes outright lies. And all of this faulty evidence played a strong and sometimes dominant role in the raging and bitter controversy that ensued.

The primary and overwhelming question remained unanswered: Was Travis Walton truly snatched out of the forest by spacemen from another world, or was he not?

To find the answer, it was at least necessary to start at the beginning. And in the beginning was Travis Walton's story—all of it, as he told it, the story that he insisted was absolutely true.

6.

Travis Walton's Story

"We were leaving work, a little after six o'clock. And as we were driving out of there, driving up the road, we saw a light coming through the trees, off to our right. I didn't know what it was. I think Allen was the first one to point it out. Steve Pierce said he thought it was a crashed airplane hanging in the trees, maybe.

"I just thought it might be the light of some hunter's camp there—headlights, or maybe a cooking fire. But we could see the light coming through there. There was a thicket in the way, and we could see the light coming onto the road ahead, kind of coming through the thicket. When we got around the thicket to where we could see, there it was.

"Mike slammed on the brakes. I threw open the door and I got out of the truck and started toward it to see it up close. It was a saucer-shaped object, about twenty feet in diameter. It had a dome on top of it. It was glowing this yellowish-white-golden color, and it was hovering about ten or fifteen or twenty feet off the ground.

"This slash pile was in the way, and I couldn't get directly underneath it, but I could see up to its bottom. It was really smooth. There were no hatches, or ports, or bolts, or anything showing on the bottom of it. It looked kind of like a hot metal light bulb, just glowing there.

"The guys on the truck were all hollering for me to come back. I was just being brazen. When I got up to it, I could hear a sound coming from it. It wasn't very loud, kind of like a high-pitched beep. It was going beep-beep-beep, but high-pitched. Just about then, I heard Mike, or somebody, holler, 'Get away from there!' And I looked around at them.

"When I looked back at the craft, it suddenly made a real loud noise, and it started to move, as if it were coming alive, kind of an erratic, spin-type movement. When I heard that, I jumped down behind this log sticking out of the slash pile right there. And I made up my mind right there that I was going to get the hell out of there. I stood up, and as I turned to go I just felt this shock, just a numbing shock. It kind of made me feel like I went numb all over. It was like the feeling you get in your hands when you hit something real hard with a baseball bat, and it kind of rings. It was kind of an electric shock, and kind of like a blow, too—like I'd been hit with a baseball bat. It all happened real fast. And I went out.

"I don't know what happened after that, but when I woke up I was laying on my back. There was a light about three feet above me, real close, and I just got the idea that I must be lying on a table, or something. At first I couldn't focus my eyes too well, and I had a lot of pain—in my head and chest mainly, but all over. I had an ache in my head and chest, but it felt kind of like a burn and an ache at the same time, all over. I felt like I was burned, inside and out, and I ached all over, too, like I'd been crushed.

"I kept going in and out. When I regained consciousness, I could hear movements around me. So I looked and saw these three creatures standing there. I just came unglued right there; I just became hysterical. I didn't know what they were doing when I woke up. I didn't know if they were examining me, or what. I was hysterical, and I had this pain, and seeing them . . . it was just terrible from then on.

"They were short, shorter than five feet, and they had very large, bald heads, no hair. Their heads were domed, very large. They looked like fetuses. They had no eyebrows, no eyelashes. They had very large eyes—enormous eyes—almost all brown, without much white in them. The creepiest thing about them were those eyes. Oh, man, those eyes, they just stared through me. Their mouths and ears and noses seemed real small, maybe just because their eyes were so huge.

"I jumped up, screaming at them. And this thing fell off my chest. It was like a thick plastic strap or something that went halfway around my chest. I didn't know what it was. When it hit the floor, it rocked back and forth, and a light came from beneath it. But there weren't any wires or tubes attached to it. It just rocked on the floor, shining underneath it.

"When I jumped up, I hit this one creature on my right, pushed him back, and he fell real easy into the next one. They had this white, marshmallowy-looking skin, and their bodies were real lightweight. When I pushed them, their bodies fell back easy. They were wearing loose coveralls, kind of an orangish-tannish-brown, gathered at the sleeves. I didn't see any zippers, no buttons, no insignia, no belt.

"I couldn't stand up very well. I kind of staggered back against the wall. There was a bench there, a narrow shelf, low to the floor, attached to the wall about two and a half feet off the floor. I grabbed this clear tube from it. I think it was a tube. It looked like it was made of glass, or some kind of clear material, about eighteen inches long. I grabbed it and tried to break the end off it; I wanted to get something sharp to defend myself with. It was too light for a club.

"They started toward me, and when that tube wouldn't break off, I just lashed out at them with it. I was screaming at them, stuff like: 'Get away from me! What are you? What's going on here?' I was just completely hysterical. They just stopped. They didn't try to attack me or anything. They didn't come real close to me. They just stopped and kind of thrust their hands out, like they meant no, or stop, or I don't know what.

"Then, all at once, they all just turned around and walked out, hurried out, shoo! They just took off. They were gone. I was afraid they'd come back.

"I looked around this room. It was really hot. The air was so wet and heavy I could hardly breathe. It was hot and dimly lit. And my mind was just raging the whole time. I could see I was inside a room, small at the end where the door was. It was like a trapezoid. That shelf had a bunch of things on it: some chrome-looking things, a couple of black squares, and this round thing, shaped like a hamburger, or yo-yo, with a piece of metal disk sticking out of one side, sideways. I didn't know what that stuff was, or if they had been using it on me.

"I was afraid that they'd come back. So after a couple of minutes I went to the door and looked down the way they had gone. It was a hallway that curved. It went to the left and to the right. They had gone right, so I went down to the left. I couldn't see anybody, so I just took off, running. I ran right past one door on the left. I wanted to find a way out, but I was just hysterical. That's the one thing I had in my mind: get out of there. I was kind of claustrophobic, hysterical. I just took off and ran, and I kind of caught the idea that there was a door there on the left, but I didn't look in.

"But I finally got hold of myself a little and told myself to check out the next door. There was one on the right there, open. So I ran up to it, then stopped. I didn't see anybody, so I went in. It was just a round room with nothing in it except a metal chair. It was just a chair with one center leg, and it sat in the middle of the room. It was high-backed, with the back to me, and I was afraid there might be someone sitting in it. So I kind of sidled along the wall until I could get a look into the chair. And a real funny thing happened.

"When I got closer to the middle of the room, it got darker in there. And when I stepped back, it got lighter again. When it got darker, I could see the stars. I could see them through the walls, through the ceiling, through the floor—everywhere. Everywhere I looked, I could see the stars, projected on the walls or through the walls. They were just there, everywhere.

"There was nobody sitting in the chair. On the right armrest, there was a panel of buttons and a small green screen with black lines across it. The left armrest had a lever on it. I wanted to find a way out of there. Across the room, there were some rectangles on the wall, flush, just cracks, really, like they might be doors. I thought if I pushed the right buttons, I could open the doors and get out.

"So I punched a couple of the buttons. Nothing happened. Then I moved the lever on the other armrest—and the stars started moving all around. The black lines on the green screen moved. The stars were rotating, but they stayed in their same positions relative to each other. They stayed in their same patterns. The patterns of stars just all moved together, through the walls and everywhere.

"That upset me. I didn't know what was going on. But I quit doing that. I was afraid I would really mess something up. I could really hurt myself doing that, playing with fire. I just decided not to do that anymore.

"Then pretty soon I heard a sound behind me. I turned around, and there was a man standing there near the door. He was a man just like a human being —not exactly Caucasian, but like a dark, evenly tanned Caucasian. He was human enough, so if I was walking down the street in a crowd, he'd be an unusual-looking person in passing. He was a big man, over six feet, and built heavy. He was wearing tight blue coveralls, with a helmet over his head.

"He motioned me over with his right hand, and I ran up to him, screaming stuff like: 'How'd you get in here? How do I get out? What is this?' I thought he could be American, just people as far as I could tell. But he didn't answer me. This helmet on his head was like a clear bubble, plastic or glass, and it was flattened on top. It had a heavy black rim that sat down low and tight on his shoulders. There weren't any hoses, or wires, or anything on it. He didn't answer me, so I thought maybe he couldn't hear me. I knew I was making sounds, because I could hear myself.

"He just kind of smiled, a tolerant grin, and he took me by the arm and led me out of there. I thought, well, I'll go with him, and maybe we'll get someplace where he'll take that helmet off, and I can talk to him where he can hear me. There was something funny about his eyes. They were kind of a strange bright golden hazel, but a lot like our eyes, too.

"We went down that hallway and through some empty space. I guess it was kind of an airlock thing. I thought we were outside. The air just got cooler, it got fresher. It just felt like out of doors. And the light was much brighter. It was like sunlight, except it was inside a big high-ceilinged room, either a building or part of a larger craft. I felt really relieved to be out of that dimly lit place, out of that heavy heat, and I could breathe again.

"We were in this building, or larger craft, that had a high curved ceiling. It was shaped like a quarter of a cylinder on its side. The roof curved down into one wall, and there were two flat walls. There were maybe two, maybe three, craft parked in there. I could see something, part of one, past the other two. They were rounded, oval, and saucer-shaped, but they didn't have any angles to them. They were smoother and shinier than the one in the woods.

"He took me out of that room, and down a hallway to another room, a smaller room. There were some other people in there, a lot like him. He put me on a chair and went out another door across the room without saying a word or making any sound at all.

"There were two men and a woman in there. They all looked like each other. They weren't twins, but they all looked like they were from the same family. They all had a family resemblance. These weren't wearing any helmets. They had the same color eyes, bright golden hazel. Their hair was long, kind of dirty blond. The woman's hair was long, and the men's hair was long enough to cover their ears. They all wore the same tight blue coveralls. The material looked soft.

"I sat in the chair talking to them. I thought maybe they could hear me, because they didn't have any helmets on. I tried to talk to them, but they wouldn't answer me, either. I kept asking them a bunch of questions, trying to get them to talk to me. But they just kind of smiled at me. Their expressions hardly changed. They never made a sound. Their faces were kind of blank. Their mouths didn't open.

"Then the woman and one of the men came over

to the chair and took me by the arms, one on each arm. They got me up and took me over to a table and started to put me on the table. At first I cooperated; I was going along with it. But they wouldn't answer my questions. If they weren't going to answer my questions, I wanted to know what was going on here.

"I started to struggle. I started to resist, yelling, 'Hey, hang on there a second! What do you think you're doing?' I don't know what else. I was just getting hysterical again.

"They just smiled, tolerant, like I was misbehaving or something. They weren't mad or anything. They had me on the table, and I was fighting back, screaming, and they just sort of smiled without really changing expression, not making a sound. And one of them reached up and started to pull down a mask, like an oxygen mask. And they tried to pull it down over my face. I reached up to pull it off, and I went out. I just lost consciousness. . . .

"That's the last thing I knew until I woke up on the highway outside of Heber. It was dark, and I was lying on my back on the pavement, and I saw one of those round craft hovering about four feet over the highway. It was hovering there for just a second. I looked up just as a light went out, like a hatch closing, or just a light going out. A white light just went off on the bottom of it. The craft was dark, and it wasn't giving off any light at all.

"And then it just shot straight up. I don't see how anything could move that fast, and not just shriek through the air. It didn't make a sound. It was just gone.

"I recognized the road; it was the highway out of Heber to Phoenix. It was about ten miles away from where I had last been in the woods. I was really relieved when I saw that thing go and I saw where I was.

"I ran down to the phone booths at the gas station there. There are three in a row. The first phone I tried didn't work. It was out of order, or something, and I started to panic again. I got hysterical, thinking that maybe none of the phones would work.

"I tried the second one, and it worked. I don't

remember how I made the call. I had change in my pocket, but you don't need money for those phones. You just pick them up and the operator is there. I don't remember dialing or calling collect. But the call went through. I called my brother-in-law because he was the only one in the family with a phone at that time. He didn't believe it was me. He said something like, 'Sorry, but you must have the wrong number,' and he started to hang up. But I screamed at him. I don't remember what I said, I was so hysterical. And finally he said, okay, he'd come for me. He said, 'I'll get your brother and we'll come get you.'

"Then I just went down to the floor. I slumped down in the booth, just thinking about it. I couldn't get those eyes out of my head. They were big glassy eyes, just all brown, with hardly any white in them. And when they blinked, it was real striking. It was like big shades on a window going up and down. They seemed to stare at you. I didn't want to look at them, and at the same time I couldn't avoid them, either.

"I was really tired, and really thirsty, but I didn't hurt so much anymore. I just burned and ached a little bit. It was a little lingering pain, but not anything like it had been at first. I just stayed there thinking about it until Duane and Grant came. They found me stuffed down in the phone booth.

"I was really happy to see them. I was really relieved. But I was still very upset, in an emotional turmoil. I wasn't groggy or anything; I was fully conscious, but I was kind of whirling in my head. Then when Duane told me how long I had been gone . . . that just blew me away.

"I could remember pretty much everything that had happened. But I thought it was all about two hours. I couldn't understand what had happened to the five days. After that, I was too upset to discuss it—with Duane, or anybody.

"I was pretty frightened. . . ."

7.

AND SO, ONCE AGAIN, HE DISAPPEARED. BUT THIS TIME there was nothing extraterrestrial about his disappearance.

On the day after Sheriff Gillespie's interrogation, Travis and Duane secretly moved into the Sheraton Hotel in Scottsdale, compliments of the *National Enquirer,* and under the protective wing of APRO. Thus hidden away, Travis was beyond the clamoring reach of reporters and UFO investigators alike.

For one, Ground Saucer Watch Director Bill Spaulding was furious. Reporters had already found Spaulding to be a most willing commentator on any facet of the case. Now he told the press, "There are some holes in this story. Duane accused us of being negative after we questioned him about a couple of those holes in the story. In the first place, this is not the way abduction victims go about things. We have many studies of past abductions, and this doesn't follow. We have some questions related to this so-called abduction. I'm not saying that I don't believe the guy. I'm just saying that he must be scientifically evaluated. The thing that is at stake is the scientific community, with respect to the entire UFO subject. Before anybody can say that this is a hoax, or that this is the real thing, the proper scientific tests must be conducted. I, of all people, would like to see this turn out to be positive. But the only way it can be done is with competent scientific personnel conducting scientific tests."

Spaulding did not describe exactly what holes he espied in Travis Walton's story, and the bulk of his public statements falsely implied that Travis might be deliberately refusing scientific examination. For even as he spoke, two of the Western world's most renowned UFO investigators were on their way to Phoenix to test and evaluate the incredible story.

One was Dr. James Harder, APRO's director of research, and professor of civil engineering at the University of California, an expert who had once been consulted by the American Congress during its 1968 investigation into the possible nature and origin of Unidentified Flying Objects.

The other was Dr. J. Allen Hynek, director of the Center for UFO Studies, chairman of Northwestern University's Department of Astronomy, and former consultant to the Air Force's UFO investigation known as Project Blue Book.

Though Harder and Hynek had worked closely together in several previous major investigations, they were unwittingly thrown into a competing situation in the Walton case. Since APRO had been chosen to take over from Spaulding's GSW, Harder was in, and Hynek was out, because Spaulding was also a field investigator for Hynek's Center for UFO studies.

Spaulding was furious. He hotly told the press that Duane Walton had refused to let his brother speak to Hynek. "First he agreed to a meeting, and then he changed his mind. This is just too much. We're going to blow this story out today."

Duane replied that Spaulding was "a publicity seeker and a glory hunter." And he pointed out that Spaulding had considered the case sound and legitimate until he was removed from it in the aftermath of his unsuccessful medical arrangements with Dr. Lester Steward.

Meanwhile, Dr. Harder quietly began his investigation. He found Travis extremely upset and tense. In Travis' words, he was "really wired, ready to crack up." So Dr. Harder decided that regressive hypnosis was immediately in order. If the story was true, Travis, in a trance, would recall it in complete detail, and the detailed recounting under hypnosis would also allow him to relive the experience without the intense fear then associated with the conscious memory of the events.

So Dr. Harder placed Travis in a hypnotic trance, and he regressed him to the time of the alleged UFO encounter and abduction. It was the first time that anyone had heard the full story. Travis recounted all the details, stored in his memory, of what had happened. And still, the complete story only accounted for about two hours of the missing five days. Nonetheless, Dr. Harder concluded, if hypnosis was indeed a truth test, Travis had passed with flying colors. He was telling the truth, as far as he knew it. He had been taken from the woods in a UFO, exactly as the six witnesses had been claiming since the outset. Apparently, the reason why Travis could not recall the entire experience—all five days of it—was because he had not been conscious for the whole time . . . or he had been hypnotically programmed not to remember anymore.

Thus, in Dr. Harder's expert opinion, Travis Walton had indeed been snatched by spacemen from another world.

Upon being awakened from the hypnotic trance, Travis expressed enormous relief. He profusely thanked Dr. Harder for exorcising the bedeviling fright that he had been suffering. Nevertheless, he was still disturbed by the missing time, and he soon lapsed back into tense agitation.

The police polygraph test was scheduled for the next day, Friday, November 14. It was to be given by Cy Gilson, of the Arizona Public Safety Department. Sheriff Gillespie had agreed to abide by the Waltons' sole condition—no one, especially the press, was to be told that the test was being given.

Dr. Harder advised against the test, saying it was premature, that Travis was not ready for it. The *National Enquirer*, which was paying the bills, was also opposed to the test. The *Enquirer* wanted an exclusive story, and *Enquirer* editors wanted their own polygraph test to be part of that exclusive.

Nevertheless, the Waltons had already consented to undergo police polygraph examination, and Cy Gilson had been forewarned by Sheriff Gillespie to keep the test as secret as possible so that Travis would not be spooked by the reporters.

On Friday morning, Gilson discovered that the press was tailing him. He went out a back door at headquarters, jogged his car around roads, stopped for a while to ensure that he had lost his tails, and then proceeded to the same place where he always gave polygraph tests. One television crew had a camera set up in an office window in the building across the way. And at the police conference that morning, the press had been advised that the lie test would be given that day. Within minutes, a reporter called Duane Walton's house and asked what time they were all coming down to take the lie tests.

Predictably, Duane Walton exploded. There weren't going to be any lie-detector tests, and if anyone wanted to know why, they could go ask Sheriff Gillespie, because he was the one who blew it by breaking the promised guarantee of secrecy.

"We agreed to the test. In fact, we asked for it," Duane said. "And we asked of the sheriff only that there be no publicity. We have had enough publicity. The sheriff broke his pact with us. And the test is off, period."

Duane's blame was wrongly placed. The agreement had certainly been broken, but not by the weary sheriff, who was by then just plain damned sick and tired of the whole damned mess. He wished aloud that the whole damned thing had happened in somebody else's county.

For the moment, he was washing his hands of the entire affair. But, if at some future date, somebody was able to prove that a hoax had been perpetrated, the hoaxers were going to be prosecuted on every charge that he could make stick, including creation of public mischief—and the perpetrators would pay every cent of expense incurred by the investigation, most notably more than ten thousand dollars expended on the search for Travis Walton in the Turkey Springs woods.

The sheriff trudged home to Holbrook and went to bed.

The next day a front-page headline in the Phoenix Gazette proclaimed:

UFO CASE IS LINKED TO DRUGS BY EXPERT

The expert turned out to be the redoubtable Dr. Lester Steward; and the drug link was forged from less than cast-iron evidence.

The newspaper story stated:

81

One of two persons known to have interviewed an alleged "space traveler" has labeled the entire incident phony and charges it was drug-related.

Dr. Lester H. Steward, director of the Modern Hypnosis Instruction Center in Phoenix, told the Phoenix *Gazette* in an exclusive interview that Travis Walton's story about being abducted into a flying saucer "is an absolute hoax."

"He [Walton] was out hallucinating on some drug, probably LSD," Steward said. "I can take you to Twenty-fourth and Van Buren [the Arizona State Hospital] and show you these types. I work with them, and I say this is a hoax."

Steward said he spent two hours with Walton and his brother Duane on Tuesday morning in his office in the Westward-Ho Motel.

The Waltons appeared at his office, Steward said, at about nine-thirty A.M., supposedly for hypnosis experiments.

They stalled the hypnotist by demanding medical attention for Travis, but they refused to leave his office to go to a lab.

"They wanted a complete physical, and they wanted it for free," Steward said. "It was like they were looking to me to provide them with some financial assistance."

But when Steward arranged the medical exam and the funds, he said, the Waltons left his office hurriedly, and the only contact he has had with them since has been two telephone conversations with Duane.

During the two-hour session, Steward said, Travis related his story about the alleged abduction near Heber.

Steward said Travis told about waking up in a white room with four "snow-white, tall, angular, but not muscular" beings looking at him. They had "misshapen heads, bulging eyes, and no fingernails," and they would not answer Travis' questions, according to the story.

"He said he swung his arms and finally got off the table upon which he was lying," Steward said. "He saw a piece of plastic pipe and wrenched it free, tried to break it over the table, then started swinging it at the creatures.

"He said they backed out and left him alone. They were wearing silvery uniforms. After they left he went out the door, down a hall-way, and into another room, where he saw a chair with buttons on the side.

"He sat down, he said, and started playing with the buttons and saw a big screen and all sorts of stars. A guy came in, a dark-haired human, and took him by the elbow into another room, where two men and a woman were standing. He said they were very nice looking. They sat him in a chair, and he said that is all he remembers."

Steward said Duane Walton called him Tuesday about regressive hypnosis because Steward is a consultant for Ground Saucer Watch, and the Walton family had been contacted Sunday by GSW's director, Bill Spaulding, at the site of the alleged disappearance.

The hypnosis never came off, Steward said, and he believes the reason is that the Waltons fear exposure.

Steward challenged the alleged infallibility of the lie-detector tests administered to the six witnesses. Five reportedly passed, but Steward said he would be unconvinced that they were telling the truth unless they went through regressive hypnosis.

"The polygraph is only a machine, and I think they got together and beat it," he said. "But they can't beat hypnosis. If they [the witnesses] did go into hypnosis, they can lie, but I can show they are lying, and they can't control it.

"They're afraid of the tests," he added.

He said that Travis appeared upset at first, but he was completely calm when the two brothers left, and Steward described that reaction as symptomatic of drug abuse.

"They didn't know that I also teach drug abuse at Maricopa Tech when they got here," Steward said, adding that their decision to leave came shortly after they learned of his background.

In another development, Spaulding said GSW headquarters had ordered him to "drop the case" immediately. Spaulding said his organization took a more-than-usual interest in the situation because of the six witnesses who reported the incident on November 12, and because he had personally found heavy magnetic traces at the scene.

However, after Duane Walton canceled an interview with Dr. Alan Hynek, of Northwestern University, and after neither Walton showed up for a lie-detector test yesterday, Spaulding said his group "has had it. We have done all we can. We will do no further investigation or spend any more money."

Spaulding said his group feared that scientific study of UFOs would suffer severely if any further action were taken in the matter here. . . .

The newspaper story was symptomatic of journalism's frantic approach to the Travis Walton story. Reporters from the press television, and radio were all in a race to rush to print with anything that anybody would say regarding the Waltons and the alleged UFO abduction. They seldom paused to corroborate the "evidence" presented in their news pieces.

Thus, the *Gazette* piece, as many others, was riddled with errors, inaccuracies, distortions and falsehoods. This unfortunate happenstance was destined to characterize the media's treatment of the Walton story for many months thereafter, which only further muddied the already murky waters. The deluge of bitter accusations became almost as unbelievable as the alleged abduction itself—all of it rife with slander, libel, calumny, defamation, a veritable maelstrom of raging vituperation. And by the sheer force of the torrent, it overwhelmed the single, most important and fundamental question: Was the Walton story true, or was it false?

Journalism simply failed to enforce one of its own most basic rules: double-check every major detail for truth and accuracy.

Steward had told the *Gazette* that the Waltons came to him "for hypnosis experiments," but they refused the tests, feared them, and were afraid of exposure.

So why in the world would they have gone to him in the first place? It was an obvious question that should have been asked, given the *Gazette*'s own material, but it wasn't. The *Gazette* had failed to exercise its own normal journalistic judgment and restraint. And thereby it rendered itself blind to the major, fatal flaw in its own story: it had not checked its facts.

Thus according to the *Gazette* the UFO case was linked by an expert to drugs. The Walton story was a hoax. And it had arisen from a drug-induced hallucination. Further, the witnesses to the alleged UFO encounter had collaborated to beat the polygraph machine. Finally, the whole gang was now afraid of undergoing legitimate testing that would unmask the fraud.

The hard verifiable, concrete evidence substantiating these allegations was the lone and unsubstantiated word of one man, whose own reputed qualifications were imminently imperiled by disclosures about their source.

The facts were that the Maricopa County medical examiner's drug-screen test of Travis Walton's blood and urine had revealed not a single trace of drugs, LSD or otherwise. There were, however, reservations about those tests. First, investigators had only Duane's word that the original urine specimen had, in fact, come from Travis. Second, the follow-up tests on blood and urine taken directly from Travis could not be considered absolutely conclusive, since the samples were taken about forty-eight hours after his return—time enough for some drugs to disappear from his system. Nevertheless, the known evidence simply did not support Steward's drug charges.

Steward was also unable to verify his claim that he had fully interrogated the Waltons for two hours. Certainly, he would have needed at least that much time to poke holes in their story. But, by his own admission, the Waltons had arrived at his office at nine-thirty, and he had spent some time on the telephone trying to find a medical doctor to conduct the tests demanded by Duane.

After leaving in a huff, the Waltons stopped for breakfast. It was a thirty-minute drive from Steward's office to Duane's home in Glendale. At ten-forty-five, Coral Lorenzen reached Duane there by telephone.

Duane estimated that he and his brother had been with Steward for less than an hour, which could have accounted for the score of errors in Steward's version of Travis' story. First, he said that Travis had related the story; later he claimed that Duane had done the talking. The fact was that the Waltons had gone to Steward for medical help, sent by Spaulding, who had identified Steward as a medical doctor. They had not gone for hypnosis. Contrary to his claim, Steward had been unable to provide Travis with a doctor. Also contrary to his claim, Travis was not afraid of testing, was not avoiding it.

He had in fact "passed" one test that Steward himself claimed could not be beaten—regressive hypnosis. And he was on that very morning submitting to polygraph examination, just as he had submitted to a full and comprehensive medical examination, and just as he was shortly to submit to an entire battery of psychiatric examinations.

As for Spaulding, GSW may very well have ordered him to "drop the case," but not before the Waltons had dropped him, a circumstance that he had tried, several times, to reverse.

Meanwhile, the enormity of Steward's charges was so great that APRO decided it had better check into his qualifications, find out who he was.

His medical degree, he said, had been earned at California Western University at Santa Ana. Catalogs at the

University of Arizona listed no accredited university by that name. But a field investigator discovered that there was a California Western University—it occupied half a dozen rooms in a Santa Ana office building. It was only two years old, and one of its officials claimed that it had evolved from the U.S. International University of San Diego, which had gone out of business. The official would not discuss accreditation and he could not provide a catalog of curriculum. He claimed there was a faculty of twelve, with a student enrollment of one thousand. However, with no campus, where were all those students?

The official explained that California Western was a "tutorial university," which, APRO discovered, was a euphemism for "correspondence school."

When questioned about his medical training and experience, Steward insisted that he was, indeed, a medical doctor, but he was not licensed to practice in the United States. But the only hint of formal medical background APRO was able to uncover in Steward's past hardly entitled him to the MD's "Dr." with which he prefixed his name. Rather, he may have once served as a medic in the United States Marine Corps. Even that could not be verified with certainty.

But, for all the public knew, Dr. Lester Steward, drug expert, had blown apart Travis Walton's incredible claim of kidnapped flight aboard an alien spacecraft from another world.

In many respects, the thoroughly abnormal contents of the tale itself seemed to impart abnormality to much that touched it. It was not only the press that suffered the affliction. The public, worldwide, knew only what the press told it about the Travis Walton case, and that knowledge was faulty, because elements of the press had broken down, elements that would normally enforce self-discipline and self-control on its own reporting of events.

That defective public knowledge was further sullied by what the press was not reporting, what it itself did not know about. Facts that both supported and disputed Travis Walton's story were not divulged by people who knew about them. That failure was not the fault of the press at large.

At this point, at least two salient factors were being withheld from public knowledge. The first appeared to corroborate the validity of Travis Walton's story. The second appeared to cast a shadow of doubt across it.

Firstly, APROs professional staff and scientific consultants considered the Walton case one of the most significant and compelling ever recorded in the history of UFO phenomena because major details contained in it coincided exactly with major details of another "abduction" case that had received no publicity at all.

Just three months earlier, and a few hundred miles to the east, Air Force Sergeant Charles Moody had undergone an experience with a UFO. The creatures he reportedly encountered were precisely the same as those described by Travis. Moody was extremely reticent to reveal his story, because he feared reprisals from the U.S. Government, his employer. However, he entrusted the case to Jim Lorenzen, of APRO, on the condition that no public disclosure be made at that time. Lorenzen knew that Moody's creatures were about five feet tall, with large, bald heads, large eyes, small ears and mouths, and their bodies appeared to be lightweight. Though these creatures did communicate with Moody, "their lips did not move" at all.

The bulk of Moody's story was considerably different from Travis Walton's, but the description of the creatures in both was the same. Neither man could have "copied" from the other, because Travis Walton was still missing when Sergeant Moody first fully described his creatures to Jim Lorenzen.

In addition, Moody's saucer-shaped object was similar to the one described in the Walton story—it also had "hospital room" aspects. In addition, Moody was also escorted through the spaceship by an "elder or leader."

Moody's tale included the implanting of a post-hypnotic suggestion, which Lorenzen believed also accounted for Travis' early insistence that he did not want the police to know that he had returned and that he had to have a doctor.

Moody's entire story was finally disclosed months later —but not in the public press.

Meanwhile, the second salient factor evolved from an event that occurred on the same day that Dr. Steward's astounding revelations were announced in the Phoenix *Gazette*.

The event was a carefully concealed secret. On Saturday afternoon, November 15, at the Sheraton Hotel in Scottsdale, Travis Walton underwent a rigorous polygraph examination. The complex circumstances surrounding it did not augur well for its future role in the bewildering Travis Walton story.

8.

TRAVIS WAS ALREADY IN A VERY DISTRESSED STATE—
jumpy, moody, withdrawn. Dr. Harder told him that he
was probably too upset to take a valid lie-detector test.
The polygraph, Dr. Harder explained, was not really a lie
detector. The machine measured stress, not lies. The examiner would ask questions. If stress accompanied the
answers, the examiner interpreted the recorded stress as
an indication of lying.

Dr. Harder maintained that Travis simply had not
calmed down enough to be tested soundly. Three consulting psychiatrists concurred: Travis was already a quiver-
ing bundle of nerves. In their collective opinion, any
polygraph test given then would be meaningless and invalid. One of the psychiatrists, Dr. Jean Rosenbaum, was
a court-accepted expert in that specific field.

Still, the *National Enquirer* was anxious to have a
polygraph test included in its exclusive story. Its chief
representative, Paul Jenkins, argued that the test would
be given in strict confidence, and its results would not be
released without Travis' permission. So what could anyone lose?

Travis consented to the test. An experienced examiner
was chosen: John J. McCarthy, director of the Arizona
Polygraph Laboratory, in Phoenix. Jim Lorenzen called
McCarthy and asked him if he would be willing to participate. Considering the highly controversial nature of the
subject, could he be objective? Yes, McCarthy answered.

Dr. Harder then described Travis' disturbed state of

mind, adding that he did not think that a test given under existing conditions would be reliable. McCarthy replied that his test procedure would allow for the subject's stress and agitation. Whereupon Paul Jenkins completed the arrangements with the examiner.

McCarthy brought his equipment over to the Sheraton, set it up, and began his pre-test interview, gleaning information requisite to his eventual formulation of test questions.

Two subjects especially upset Travis. But he nonetheless volunteered information about them when McCarthy questioned him about his background. Travis revealed his participation in the theft and forgery of payroll checks from Snowflake's Western Molding Company four years before. And he candidly admitted that he had experimented with pot, uppers, and even LSD once—all when he was a teen-ager. He called his drug experimentation a "passing phase" of youth, and he swore that he had not touched any narcotics for any reason for several years.

Some antagonism between Travis and McCarthy resulted from the pre-test interview. To some observers, McCarthy at times seemed to be badgering, argumentative, even abusive. Even in normal situations, Travis reacted badly to hostility. Further, Travis was ashamed of his juvenile past, and talking about it, especially to strangers, upset him.

Tension was also evident during McCarthy's extensive probe into Travis' previous UFO interest. Travis admitted to some interest. He had speculated about making contact with a UFO, but he did not consider himself a UFO buff. He most certainly didn't dwell on the subject, and he had never even read a book about it. He thought his interest was normal. And he was growingly agitated by attempts to portray himself and his family as UFO freaks—since the implication was that his story was a hoax, created from long-standing zeal.

Travis said, "I've been interested in UFOs to the same degree that almost everybody is. I have not been fanatical about the subject. I'm not obsessed by it. I've talked about it, but not constantly, only rarely."

He signed a statement of consent, declaring that he was voluntarily submitting to the test, that he had been advised of his rights against self-incrimination, and that he understood that "any statement made by me may be used as evidence against me in subsequent judicial proceedings. . . ."

McCarthy promised complete confidentiality, assuring Travis that the test results would be the sole property of Paul Jenkins and the *Enquirer:* "If there's any release of the information, it will come from him, not me. The information will never leak out of this office. You can rest assured of that."

With that promise, McCarthy signed an agreement that, for the sum of three hundred dollars, "I have conducted the test in absolute secrecy and will not divulge the results to anyone but Mr. Jenkins and Mr. [John] Cathcart [associate editor of the *Enquirer*] at any time."

The test was given, and McCarthy reported the results thusly:

On November 15, Travis C. Walton was given a polygraph examination for the *National Enquirer,* at the request of Mr. Paul Jenkins, in reference Walton's recent UFO experience. The examination commenced at 1425 [two-twenty-five P.M.] and was concluded at 1615 [four-fifteen P.M.] hours.

During the examination, he showed gross deception on the charts as he answered the following relevant questions as indicated:

1). Were you actually taken aboard a spacecraft near Heber on November 5?—"Yes."

2). Were you actually in a spacecraft from the fifth to the tenth of November?—"Yes."

3). Have you lied to Dr. Harder about being in a spacecraft?—"No."

4). Have you acted in collusion with others to perpetrate a UFO hoax?—"No."

5). Did you lie to any of Sheriff Gillespie's questions concerning your disappearance?—"No."

6). Were you hiding somewhere in Arizona during your disappearance?—"No."

7). Have you been advised by anyone to lie on this examination?—"No."

His reactions on the control test were normal. He appeared to be lucid, and prior to testing he stated that he understood each of the questions to be asked and that he could answer each with a "Yes" or "No." It was obvious during the examination that he was deliberately attempting to distort his respiration pattern.

Based on his reactions on all charts, it is the opinion of this examiner that Walton, in concert with others, is attempting to perpetrate a UFO hoax, and that he has not been on any spacecraft.

According to McCarthy, Duane was furious about the results. The psychiatric experts merely restated their previous position—the test was invalid because of the conditions under which it was given. Travis was already too distressed to be examined accurately.

APRO's Jim Lorenzen vehemently criticized the test. "In his pre-test interview with Travis and in the framing of questions, McCarthy broke some of the most elementary rules of the polygraphic profession. Specifically, two significant questions were posed in terms that forced Travis to answer on the basis of assumption, rather than experience.

"To a third question in the test, McCarthy, during the pre-test interview, had created a deliberate association with an event in Travis' past of which he is ashamed.

"Polygraph test questions must be phrased in such a way that they can be answered with a simple "Yes" or "No;" thus, they must be phrased so that the subject can answer from his own experience or knowledge. McCarthy's first test question violated these simple concepts: 'Were you actually taken aboard a spacecraft near Heber on November 5?'

"Travis was boxed in. The question forced him to speculate, since the information required to answer the question was not in his memory. Experienced polygraph operators know that this situation will produce the stress reaction that they call deception. In the pre-test interview, Travis had just explained to McCarthy that he had blacked out after experiencing something like a physical blow after he had approached the UFO, and that his next memory was of being on his back in what he first thought was a hospital, and he had no idea how much time had passed in the interim.

"McCarthy's next question is no better: 'Were you actually in a spacecraft from the fifth to the tenth of November?'

"Travis has repeatedly emphasized that he did not know where he was, and that, of the five-day period, he remembers, at the most, two hours.

"There is no way that Travis, whether he said "Yes" or "No," could have passed these first two questions," Lorenzen stated.

"McCarthy claims that Travis admitted that he, his brother Duane, and his mother often speculated about riding in a UFO. The tape recording made of the interview shows that Duane and his mother were not mentioned in connection with UFO-riding, and that in response to McCarthy's repeated and persistent questioning about riding in a UFO, Travis maintained that he had merely speculated about making contact with UFO beings, not in taking a ride per se. When reviewing the question, 'In the past, have you ever thought of riding in a UFO?' " Travis decided to respond with a "Yes" because he probably had thought about it at some time or other. He explained this to McCarthy. So, once again, McCarthy had asked the wrong question.

" 'Have you recently thought a lot about riding in a UFO?' would have given a lot better indication of whether or not Travis had been planning a hoax.

"Describing this test as meaningless, as we have done, is really being too kind. It was badly botched by the tester. Sometimes long years of experience can serve to crystallize bad habits."

Dr. Harder thought that all the other evidence amply overruled the validity of the polygraph results. As he had advised prior to the test, the polygraph examination at that time was useless as scientific information, in his opinion.

Whatever the true significance, the fact that Travis had been tested and had flunked was concealed. Not even the police knew that the examination had occurred. The subsequent *Enquirer* report of its investigation of the Walton story did not mention the test. The *Enquirer* paid Travis $2,500, and $416.60 was given to each of the Rogers' crewmen. The payment was called an "award for the most scientifically valuable case of the year."

Meanwhile, Dr. Harder simply announced that Walton

was not lying about his story; it was not a hoax. His full report would be forthcoming shortly, and it would detail and analyze all the pertinent facts and theories.

One of the psychiatrists, Dr. Rosenbaum, chairman of the Southwest Psychoanalytic Association, spoke on behalf of the half a dozen experts who had investigated the case in conjunction with the *Enquirer* and APRO. His evaluation took a curious tack.

"A comprehensive battery of psychiatric and medical exams were conducted on Travis Walton," reported Dr. Rosenbaum. "And our conclusion, which was absolute, is that this young man is not lying, that there is no collusion involved. The full test results show that he really believes these things, that he is not lying.

"He really believes that he was abducted by a UFO. But my evaluation of the boy's story is that, although he believes this is what happened, it was all in his own mind. I feel that he suffered from a combination of imagination and amnesia, a transitory psychosis—that he did not go on a UFO, but simply was wandering around during the period of his disappearance. But I'm unable to account for five witnesses having the same basic story and passing lie-detector tests about it."

Since he did not believe the abduction story, he could hardly be considered biased toward Travis, thereby giving some credibility to his opinion that no polygraph test would be valid at that time. Dr. Rosenbaum's theory of temporary psychosis did not preclude the possibility that Travis had actually been felled by the blue-green shot of light from the UFO. Such physical trauma could produce the amnesiac wandering to which he ascribed Travis' disappearance. But Rosenbaum himself declined to speculate about exactly what might have triggered the psychosis.

So, two factors had to be dealt with: possible temporary psychosis, and a wandering fugue as a result of it.

Travis was given a Rorschach test by Dr. Harold Cahn, a physiologist and APRO's consultant on parapsychology. Dr. Cahn's report stated:

Travis presented a cooperative attitude toward the test situation, and, in my opinion, results are a valid indication of his basic personality structure and "overlay" due to his recent traumatic experience. Following is a précis of both features based on the test itself, and my clinical impression.

Travis presents a good, normal record, showing fair to good general intelligence, sincerity of response, and a reasonably outgoing and cooperative personality. He exhibits a good tendency to view a situation from several points of view before interpretation. He does not show rigidity, either intellectually or emotionally. There is, however, some tendency to avoid emotional aspects of a situation, which reflects a somewhat introversive personality organization. He is not highly suggestible.

Superimposed on a good, normal, basic personality structure are some fairly definite indicators of recent, and hopefully, transient malindications [bad effects] due to the recent "abduction" experience. There is a tendency toward depression and an effort to avoid full involvement in a given situation, especially if it's emotionally loaded. This is revealed by time delay and high D and DR responses, coupled with no FC, CF, and C responses on the color cards [VIII, IX, X]. Some tendency to fall back on his "nature-oriented" background is indicated.

The Minnesota Multiphasic Personality Inventory test was conducted by Lamont McConnell, a master of psychology, and interpreted by Dr. R. Leo Sprinkle, director of Counseling and Testing and associate professor of psychology at the University of Wyoming.

Dr. Sprinkle reported:

The profile [of Travis Walton] is viewed as a "normal" pattern of scores; there is no indication of a neurotic or psychotic reaction.

All items were answered; thus the Question Scale score shows no influence on other scale scores. The L Scale is within average range [Scale score equals 60]. The F Scale score [46] shows a normal reaction to the "unusual" items. The K Scale score[64] can be viewed as an indication of a heightened level of "self-awareness."

All Scale scores are within the average range, except Scale 6 [Paranoia], which shows a T score of 62. The score may be interpreted as a tendency toward skepticism or doubt; of course, the score may reflect an uncertainty about the testing situation and perceived purpose of examination.

The Ego Strength [ES] Scale score [66 T score] is an indication that the examinee scores like persons who are viewed as possessing good health, a strong sense of reality, and feelings of personal adequacy and vitality.

Conclusion

To the extent that a personality inventory is an aid in assessing the character of an examinee, the MMPI profile of Travis Walton provides a picture of a healthy young man, with a good sense of self-awareness, a tendency toward skepticism, and an inner strength of emotional stability.

The fundamental conclusion was: Travis was certifiably sane. However, the tests could not totally disprove Rosenbaum's theory, the key word of which was "temporary" psychosis. On the other hand, Rosenbaum's theory was supported by no concrete, verifiable evidence at all.

But had Travis simply been wandering around the woods for five days, amnesiac or not? The police had investigated a report that he had been seen by an elderly Snowflake couple, Mr. and Mrs. William Boring.

Boring claimed that he had seen Travis hitchhiking on a road outside Heber a day after the alleged abduction. Deputy Glen Flake was dispatched to interrogate the two witnesses. Boring was considerably more certain about what he had seen than his wife. And, in a bizarre twist of circumstance, Boring was afflicted with a speech defect that required him to speak through a mechanical voice box; the effect was a blurred metallic twang, in which exact words were difficult to understand. Boring also had to pause frequently to catch his breath. The mechanical sound was not unlike a special voice effect that might be devised for the dramatic portrayal of a being from outer space.

Boring gave his account of what had happened to Fred Sylvanus. "I was driving down the road outside Heber on that second day. . . . I saw a man exactly like the man that they said had been gone. . . . He was on my side of the road. . . . He saw my pickup and he ran to the other side. . . . He was disguised a little bit from what he is supposed to have been. . . . I know the man in Heber exactly as I saw him. . . . And as I saw him, I said to my wife, well, tonight or to-morrow night, he'll land right back in Heber—you watch what I told you. . . . And that night around eleven or twelve o'clock he did come into Heber. . . .

"This man was disguised a little bit from his natural look. . . . I know it was him. . . . I know because I have seen him ever since he's been in that town, Snow-flake, running around . . . and he's been in a little trouble, but not enough . . . never knew anything else about it. . . .

"Me and my wife were going down the road and I saw him there and I told Mom, well, Mother, he's disguised a little bit, but it looks like him. . . . Look at him. . . . He's just standing there. . . . It looks exactly like him. . . . He had his hair sticking up straight out from the top of his head. . . . And that's the way I saw him. . . . And my wife said that it looked like him. . . . And I said, well, it is only him. . . . I know it is him. . . . I know that to be a fact. . . .

"When I first saw him, he was on my side of the road. . . . And he strained, like he might be noticed, and he ran across over to the other side and started down the hill. . . . But he didn't go all the way down. . . . Then I told my wife, I said, look at him. . . . She said well, it sure looked like him. . . . He knew me, and I think I knew him. . . ."

Flake was not so sure. The Borings began arguing between themselves about details of the story. Mrs. Boring was not altogether certain that the young man she had seen was Travis. And Travis had not returned to Heber that night, or the next one, as Boring claimed. Flake did not quite buy the idea that a "disguised" Travis would be out hitchhiking on the road, where anyone might see him. The "disguise" itself further diluted the chance of positive identification. All in all, Flake tended to discount the story. There were too many holes in it, too many flaws. It had to be considered less than conclusive by the police.

When questioned about it, Travis said, "These people do not know me very well at all. They did pick me up once when I was hitchhiking, but that was four or five years ago. I have not had any occasion to speak to either of them since then. When I asked Glen Flake about it, he just laughed it off and was evidently convinced there was nothing to it. And there was an All-Points Bulletin out on me at that time, and I understand that the Heber area was, in vulgar terms, 'crawling with cops' and other searchers. If I had been out there hitchhiking, it would seem likely that others would have reported seeing me."

Boring himself remained absolutely positive in his belief that he had seen Travis Walton hitchhiking on the Heber road the day after the alleged abduction. But other evidence simply did not support the possibility that the "abductee" had been wandering around in the woods for five days, during which time the nightly temperatures had plunged to below freezing.

On November 22, Dr. Harder completed his report on the Travis Walton case. In it, he wrote:

The purpose of this report is to analyze the evidence for and against several hypotheses that have been put forward concerning the nature of the abduction case that began with the events of November 5, 1975. I will assume some familiarity with the case on the part of the readers to whom this is directed.

After outlining the basic sequence of events, and the facts that were not in great dispute, Dr. Harder turned his attention to some of the controversial test results, and then he gave his appraisal of several hypotheses:

The reports of psychiatric examinations indicate that Travis had had a childhood marked by two broken marriages for his mother and two "abandonments," one by his natural father and one by a stepfather. He had a marked interest in "flying saucers" and believed that his natural father shared his interest. He was also interested in electronics and machinery. Previous to his encounter, he had discussed an interest in "going for a ride" on a UFO, and had indicated that this could happen. His family also had an interest in some psychic phenomena, though there is no indication to my knowledge that Travis shared this interest.

On the basis of this background, at least two psychiatrists came to the conclusion that he could have imagined the events of the abduction and that he might have suffered a "temporary" psychotic break. One, at least, was careful to say that he did not offer this as a conclusion, but only as a possibility. It is interesting that this psychiatrist accepted as fact the reality of the sighting by the primary six witnesses, and did not think that Duane was lying.

Travis did not show up for a polygraph test scheduled by the Navajo County sheriff on November 14. I and several others recommended against this test on the following basis. At that time, Travis was still in a highly emotional state marked by anxiety and fear. A polygraph test measures emotional stress usually associated with lying, but which may also be associated with stressful memories. In my view, there are no neutral stress-free control questions concerning UFOs that could have been devised. Under the circumstances, then, any results of a polygraph test would have been useless or misleading. This assessment was confirmed by Dr. Jean Rosenbaum, a psychiatrist who examined Travis a day later.

A second important consideration is that in cases of this sort, the witness has usually been subjected to a strong but unremembered hypnotic-like suggestion that he will not remember parts of his experience. This would not prevent an unconscious [but sometimes very strong] reaction to questions that could easily be assumed to be lying by a polygraph operator inexperienced in UFO abduction cases.

The Hypotheses

1). The entire story is a hoax. This hypothesis

would have to explain how the six primary witnesses could pass a lie-detector test administered by a sheriff who was very skeptical and who apparently entertained a theory of conspiracy to commit murder [the report of "inconclusive" in the case of one of the witnesses was based on a single minor question, the answer to which was only relevant to feelings of hostility toward Travis].

2). The sighting by the six witnesses is factual, but Travis made up the rest of the story as a hoax. In this hypothesis, the motivation would have to be notoriety or financial. However, Travis would have to have recovered from the blow from the UFO, would have had to secrete himself for five days from the search parties, would have to have found shelter and food [to explain the lack of acetone in the urine sample], and would have to have abstained from drinking water [to have produced the dehydration].

3). Travis entered into a conspiracy with his brother and/or others to make up the part of the story concerning the abduction. This hypothesis must deal with the fact that his brother was in Phoenix at the time of the reported abduction. It also would seem to require that the UFO be a part of the conspiracy to account for the needed planning, together with a plan to keep Travis secreted, as in Hypothesis #2.

4). The events as related by Travis and his brother are true. This is supported by Travis' description of the type-B humanoids, which matches in six characteristics that of another case completely unknown to Travis. No characteristics are different in the two descriptions, including apparent weight, height, size of head, size and placement of eyes, size and placement of ears, and the nose and mouth features. This second case occurred three months previous to this case, and only a few hundred miles away. The lack of acetone and the dehydration might be explained by the minimal administration of intravenous fluids or by some advanced medical procedures. Advanced medical techniques have been reported in several other cases.

Conclusion

Only Hypothesis #4 fits with all the facts so far developed, and we must add this to the dozen or more cases of UFO abductions reported as of this date.

Without one key piece of evidence, a theoretical case could be made for Hypotheses #2, #3, or some combinaation of them both. However, with the key piece of evidence, Dr. Harder's conclusion appeared sound.

The key was the other case, in which the humanoids matched the description of the first creatures in Travis' story. Details of the case, involving Air Force Sergeant Charles Moody, were still being kept a strict secret.

But several days later, Dr. Harder again made reference to it, in a letter to Dr. Kandell:

> Several months ago, we had a case similar to that of Travis Walton in one of your nearby states, in which there was a measurable radiation damage to the victim. I am in touch with him and will be asking that he send to you a medical records release form. Unfortunately, he is in the military, and the case was handled in a military hospital. He may already have some of his records; however, we should be guided by these records, insofar as his description of the humanoids is exactly that of Travis', and Travis may have suffered some of the same radiation.

Regarding other aspects of Travis' physical condition, Harder wrote:

> I have looked up the data in another abduction case that may have some bearing on the weight loss and lack of acetone in the Walton case. It is the Higdon-Wyoming case. When first approached, the witness was offered four "four-day" pills, with the instruction that he should take one. It was inferred that the day was only ten hours long [the witness made this statement without giving a source for

thinking this], and that the effect would last forty hours. [It is interesting that Jupiter, Saturn, and Uranus all have rotation periods of between ten and eleven hours.] He took the pills about four o'clock P.M. Friday, and he was admitted to a hospital at approximately two A.M. Saturday [October 26, 1974], after having been abducted for two and a half hours. He was not hungry on Saturday, but when he woke up at eight o'clock on Sunday, he . . . was "hungry enough that I could have eaten two horses if they'd been there." The elapsed time was thus just forty hours. This calculation may have been his source of the "ten-hour" day.

What such a pill might contain is problematical— the other three were taken from him when it was decided [by the captors] that he was not what they were looking for. But [the pills] might have contained any number and kind of enzymes, some of which could have been active in breaking down acetone, and some of which could have suppressed the hunger and/or thirst reaction, or the bowel-evacuation reflex. He was told at the hospital on Sunday that his blood was "very rich," whatever that means. We could probably get his records, too.

I wonder if there is a way we could calibrate the Walton bathroom scale so we would have a better idea of the weight gain from Tuesday to Thursday. In metabolizing fat, a person with a basal rate of eighteen hundred calories per day would use up only two hundred grams of fat per day, or only one kilogram in five days. I don't know how fast one can put that back on, but it would be hard to eat so much in only one day or two. Anyway, the loss seemed to be mostly water. [Looking over the above, I note that, had he been out of doors, the calorie rate would be closer to three thousand.]

Jim Lorenzen followed up on the calibration of scales and he noted: "Walton brought in the scale and it coincided with Kandell's office scale, verifying that Travis lost eleven to twelve pounds in the five days."

Harder wanted one further test. "I hope we have blood samples adequate to make some determination of the possible radiation exposure. Do you have a friendly pathologist who could describe the needs?"

Lorenzen provided the follow-up answer. "Travis' platelet count was within normal range, which would seem to indicate that he did not receive any radiation."

Regarding the air force sergeant's case, Lorenzen observed, "The Moody radiation damage has been hard to verify. I personally saw the rash on his lower torso and upper legs, but his medical records on this have been purged, or called forward [the military answer to the Freedom of Information Act]. According to Moody's account, he was treated to a two-hour enema and a week of laxatives, and he was told that he had received a dose of radiation. We could not find any record of the treatment, although we did locate the medical doctor who treated him."

9.

ONE NIGHT, A WEEK AFTER TRAVIS WALTON'S REAPPEAR-
ance, Deputy Glen Flake was on desk duty at the sheriff's
office in Holbrook. The whole world seemed to be going
crazy over the UFO story. Calls were coming in from
England, Germany, Canada, and all the major cities in the
United States—newspapers, magazines, television. Everybody wanted to know what was going on up there in the
high-plateau country.

In the midst of the hubbub, the sheriff's station over in
Pinetop broke in on the dispatcher's radio—the deputies
were talking to each other about a strange light that was
hovering near the mountains just east of them. The light
was changing color from blue to red to white. It was just
sitting there, not moving, and it kept changing color.

Pinetop was sixty to seventy miles south of Holbrook.

Then the St. Johns sheriff's station broke in. St. Johns
was about forty miles east of Snowflake. The deputies
there were watching the same thing. It was hanging just
above the hills, and it wasn't an airplane, but nobody
could figure out what it was. It just sat there, glowing blue,
then red, then white, then back to blue again. Some of the
deputies were getting pretty excited.

So Flake went outside and took a look, and he could
see it, too, the same thing the other deputies were talking
about. It was just sitting in the middle of this triangle of
sheriffs' stations, not going anyplace, and it changed color
every few seconds. A few more deputies joined Flake,
watching it, and they agreed that it could not possibly be
an airplane; they wouldn't be able to see a plane that far

away, and the plane lights would be different. Besides, if it were a plane, somebody within the triangle of watchers would be in a position to see the plane moving across the sky.

Flake returned to the desk to answer the phones. About then he got a call from Boston or Chicago, a newspaper or television man—all such distinctions had become thoroughly blurred by then. The man said, "Have you seen any more UFOs?" He was kind of laughing.

And Flake said, "Sure. We're watching one right now."

The man nearly fell over. "What's it doing? What's it doing?" So Flake told him. Very excited, the man said, "Go out and see if it's still there!"

Flake went out, and it was still there, so he returned and told the man.

"Well, what is it?" he wanted to know, beside himself.

"I don't know what it is," Flake replied, laconic. "It's just there, and it's not moving, and it wasn't there before. You tell me what it is."

The Holbrook deputies watched it for about thirty minutes, then just got tired of watching it, went back inside, and forgot about it.

Glen Flake, for one, had long since gotten used to seeing the unusual up there in the vast open range of the nighttime skies.

So had a lot of other people who lived high up on the plateau prairie, like Jim Carter, of Taylor. A year before, he had been working on the Salt River Electrification Project, drilling water holes on the Glen Flake ranch, about ten miles out of Snowflake, on the road to Holbrook. The drillers were working at night. One night, all of a sudden, a bright light popped on right above the drilling rig. It lit up the whole area. The men all looked up, startled. Some kind of very big object was hovering right overhead. But it was so bright that they had to shield their eyes from the glare of it, and they couldn't see what it was.

It scared the hell out of them. The thing just sat there for two or three minutes. And then, just as abruptly as it had appeared, it was gone. It rose up, the light popped off, and it was gone, vanished without a sound or sign of it anywhere in the blackened sky.

The men stood there, dumbfounded, jabbering at each

other, wondering what had happened. Seconds later a car came racing down the dirt road from the highway. It screeched to a halt at the drill tower and the foreman jumped out, all in a tizzy, but trying to act casual.

"Did you . . . uh . . . fellas see what I just saw?" he asked.

They excitedly affirmed that they had. What was it, anyway?

"I don't know what in the world it was," the foreman replied. "But I'm damned glad you saw it, too. If you hadn't seen it, I never would have said a word about it. You'd have thought I was crazy."

Carter often watched for *them* afterward, and he saw *them* again. He asked the Flakes if he could go down to their ranch at night and watch *them*, and they said sure, go ahead. Sometimes they went out by the creek to watch for the things themselves. They seldom saw *them* closer than about a half mile off, and they never tried to explain exactly what it was they were seeking. But they certainly knew that they were seeing something that was more than just passing odd.

Just about the time of the drilling tower incident, another event occurred, strange and unexplained. One evening, toward sundown, Rue Hunt was driving the high school activity bus from Snowflake to Heber. He was driving a dozen or so football players home from practice when a commotion broke out about something hanging over a farm field just off the highway to their left. Hunt stopped the bus and they all trooped off to get a better look.

A large flying object was hovering over the field, about two hundred yards south of the highway. It was cigar-shaped and glowing, about the size of an airliner, and it was hovering in mid-air, about as high as a tree would be. It was an astounding sight, just hanging there and glowing. Some of the kids got a little shook up by the sight of it.

And as they were watching, it suddenly shot straight up and disappeared in a streak of silence. It was just gone, in a second, without a trace.

Rue Hunt was not the kind of man to be out telling tall tales, Glen thought, about UFOs or anything else. And those boys saw it, too. In fact, some folks around Snowflake believed that a lot more people had seen UFOs thereabouts than would admit to it.

Nobody likes being ridiculed for being a nut and a kook. One utterly respectable matron, whose car was "just turned right off" by one, confided, "There is no way that I'm going to tell people about it, so they can say I was out hallucinating on drugs at night. I'd die if that ever got around. But what happened happened. I was driving down to Payson, and this light came on over the car. I couldn't see what it was. But the car cut off, and the headlights went out, and we just sat there, stopped. We just waited. What else could we do? These days, everything in a car is power steering and such. When it goes off, you don't go anywhere. But, pretty soon, this light took off . . . and the car worked fine again. It started right up."

Glen Flake accepted the stories as truth, because the people telling them were good, honest, reliable people. They weren't nuts, they weren't drinkers—they were just seeing something they couldn't explain. And they were seeing things that a lot of people had seen.

His brother, Sank Flake, also knew the stories: the Rue Hunt story; the Holbrook–St. Johns–Pinetop deputies watching the light; the drillers' account. Bill Estes had been chased in his car by a lighted object. The light swooped overhead, hovering, and the car stopped dead. When the thing took off, the car worked fine again.

Boyd Gardner (Glass & Electric) and C. R. Hatch (Saw & Cycle) were followed by one. But their car didn't shut off. They raced home and ran into the house. Through the window, they could see it sitting out there, like it was waiting for them to come out. One of their wives went out, and the thing just took off, disappeared.

Sank himself had been chased by one when he was just a boy. He was working the green-chain (late) shift at the Heber paper mill. It was just before dawn, and he was driving home from work with a buddy when they saw a very bright light rise up over the trees on the ridge behind them. It acted like it was following them, and it scared the wits out of them. They raced home to wake up their families and tell them. It followed them all the way home. Sank was petrified.

But after he calmed down, he told himself that it had only been a star, he was sure. He was convinced that it was just a star. It only looked like it had been chasing them. He even got up early on some mornings to watch for the lights, and that's what he saw—a star, the Rising Star, the Morning Star, some planet ascending.

He decided that *they* were just things that happened everywhere, all the time, weren't they? They were just things that people see everywhere. He didn't doubt the stories; he believed most of the storytellers were truthful —they saw something lighted up, that seemed to fly, and it was unexplained. But people were seeing stars, or they were mistaken about what they were seeing. They weren't seeing flying saucers or spaceships from other worlds. Some of them just believed that they were.

And that's what he thought Travis Walton had taken advantage of—people's belief in UFOs. Sank didn't believe in UFOs, and he didn't believe Travis Walton's story, either.

But other people did. And perhaps that belief accounted for a long series of sightings throughout the area, most lately around Springerville, Pinetop, and McNary. In both Pinetop and McNary, farmers reported finding cattle inexplicably mutilated in their fields at the same time that UFOs had been reported overhead.

Perhaps warped minds were simply taking advantage of the bizarre Walton episode or its predecessors. UFO sightings and cattle mutilations had coincided in several Western states for several years. But no one had ever been able to forge a definite link between the two happenstances. An especially grotesque string of such mutilations had occurred north in Colorado, spooking even veteran lawmen.

Typically, a large bright object would appear in the sky, rotating red, green, and white lights. Shortly thereafter, small lighted objects would fly out of the belly of the larger light, nicknamed Big Mamma, and streak away. About an hour and a half later, the lights would all rendezvous and Big Mamma would suddenly disappear in a great burst of speed.

The next day, mutilated cattle would be discovered in nearby fields. Vital organs were surgically removed from each one of them: eyes, ears, nose, anus, bladder, uterus —without any signs of bleeding, without any human tracks around them, without any disturbance to the rest of the herd. Sometimes whole animals were simply drained of all blood.

The precision and skill with which the surgery was performed astounded investigating veterinarians. Some of the excisions were managed without leaving a single scalpel cut on any of the surrounding flesh.

At first, lawmen theorized that the mutilations were the work of religious kooks or sadistic cultists engaged in some bizarre ritual. But the lights in the sky changed their minds. Thus, even before pod marks were found on the ground near several of the mutilations, perfectly sober and responsible sheriffs simply concluded that something from the lights was responsible.

In less than two years, nearly eighty such cases were reported, and estimates placed the unreported cases in the hundreds.

Scores of reputable and reliable witnesses observed Big Mamma and the smaller brightly lighted objects that flew out of her belly. Cars chased them, and so did planes. Photographs were taken. Evidence was accumulated and analyzed. Still, nothing substantial beyond the basic fact was ever learned: UFOs and mutilations appeared to be linked. How and why were not discovered.

But, curiously, the beginning of these baffling events occurred in August, 1975—precisely coincidental with the alleged "spacenapping" of Sergeant Charles Moody.

Thereafter, the incident of UFO sightings and cattle mutilations increased significantly, spreading as far north as Wisconsin.

Thus, on November 4, 1975, the day before a UFO allegedly kidnapped Travis Walton, a sheriff's deputy in Fennimore took photographs of a large bright light swinging to and fro in the sky west of town. Nearby, a farmer in Patch Grove, reported that a ball of fire was hovering atop a hill, lighting up the whole valley. Other witnesses also reported seeing unidentified lights flying around Posten's farm.

And the next day a five hundred-pound Holstein was found dead, with its left ear and tongue cut off. An investigating veterinarian decided that something seemed to have frightened the cow, causing it to run berserk, until "it developed emphysema in its lungs" and just dropped dead. "The cuts were probably made after death, because there wasn't much blood around them," he said, not overly convinced that he could explain the incident at all.

All of this was the stuff on which twisted imaginations might have preyed around Pinetop and McNary. But maybe it wasn't. The UFOs were reported, and the cattle were mutilated. What caused either, or both, was not known. Nor was it known what caused a triangular sighting of UFOs sixty miles north of Holbrook three months before the alleged Walton encounter, at the same time as Moody's experience. The evidence, however, was stark, and unlike the product of someone's crippled mind fabricating demonic artifice.

It began at ten-twenty-three P.M. on August 17, 1975, in the joint-use Navajo-Hopi Indian reservation area. A police officer, driving a Ford Bronco patrol van near Keams Canyon, was startled by a brilliant white light appearing suddenly behind him. Abruptly, the whole area lit up.

The officer slowed down, turned, and saw a dark flying object, mounted by red, green, and white lights. The lights obscured his view of the object itself.

He stopped the van, got out, and the area immediately became totally dark. The lights were gone; the object was gone. Shortly thereafter, the officer resumed his patrol.

About four minutes later, the patrol van went haywire: the engine cut off, the headlights went out, and the two-way radio went dead. All electrical systems failed. In UFO terminology, the van had suffered total EME—electromagnetic effects.

Less than sixty seconds later, the van's lights popped on, the engine started, and the officer reported the incident over his now-functioning two-way radio. The report was logged on the police record.

Just twenty-five minutes later and thirty miles north, near Pinon, three officers reported unidentified flying objects traveling at low altitude south of them. There were two objects, flashing red and green rotating lights, bisected by a bright white "spotlight." Within minutes, the objects seemed to streak out of sight, or just disappeared.

Almost immediately thereafter, four flashing objects appeared at about five thousand feet in the direction of Keams Canyon. The objects were flying in a rectangular formation, and they seemed to be changing color, from red to green to white. The officers could not relate what they were watching to anything they had ever seen in the area before.

Then, sixty miles west, at Tuba City, both policemen and citizens reported seeing brightly lighted objects streaking at tremendous speeds across the sky. Subsequent investigations by both police and Ground Saucer Watch representatives revealed: high residual magnetic traces on the back and roof of the Bronco patrol van; burn spots in the scrub brush near the first sighting; no faulty mechanical parts that could have contributed to the normal breakdown of the van's electrical systems. The witnessing officers were all considered experienced and reliable.

Responding to official queries, Luke Air Force Base, in Arizona, and Holloman, in New Mexico, reported having flown no aerial missions that could have caused the sightings in the joint-use area that night. And, according to GSW, "The profile of the sightings does not lend itself to natural or celestrial phenomena. Additionally ruled out were weather balloons, birds, space decay, [known space] objects, or any White Sands rocket launchings."

The triangle formed by the sighting areas of Tuba City, Pinon, and Keams Canyon was almost identical to the size and shape of the triangle formed by Holbrook, St. Johns, and Pinetop—the points from which the mysterious red-blue-white "UFO" was observed by sheriffs' deputies exactly three months later and in the aftermath of the Travis Walton "abduction" case.

Was all, or any of it, related? The answer was that nobody knew—at least, nobody supplied an answer to the puzzling question. However, as the sheer bulk of cases grew, as the seemingly corroborated evidence piled up, thoroughly rational (sometimes even skeptical) people were not ashamed to admit that something quite incredible seemed to be going on. What it was, they didn't know, nor why. But it was becoming increasingly difficult to block out the riddle in the skies by simply raising a hand across their blinking eyes.

One large piece of the riddle was the story of Air Force Sergeant Charles Moody, who was allegedly abducted from a New Mexico desert just three months before the alleged Walton abduction and less than three hundred miles southeast of Turkey Springs.

Actually, "desert" does not accurately describe the land from which Moody was allegedly taken by creatures from another world. Instead, it is a land shouldered by husky mountain ranges, like the San Andres and the Sierre Oscura—home of the White Sands Missile Range and Test Center, and headquarters of Holloman Air Force Base, respectively.

The highest peak is Sierra Blanca, which rises twelve thousand feet into the vast New Mexico sky. Awesome, Sierra Blanca is the ancient guardian of the Mescalero Apache Indians, whose reservation spreads away from the shadows of the protective peak. High up in the peak, the Mescalero Apache believe, live the spirit creatures from another world, spirits who come from the sky, and the sun, and the stars. They were the gods who were first, and who were always, and who are—the Elders, who are not mortal men, but who are the ancestors that soared down from beyond.

It is a belief that re-echoes, with only slight variation, throughout the tribal lore of all the Indian nations of Arizona and New Mexico—the Apache, the Navajo, the Hopi, the Pueblo, and the Zuni. It is sacred lore that has been passed down through thousands of years of generations, traversing all tribal cultures—even those rooted in times before Christianity was known in the world.

One of those cultures was the Mogollon, which gave its name to the rugged mountains that lock together eastern Arizona and western New Mexico. The Mogollon is the land bridge connecting the Travis Walton "abduction" site to that of Sergeant Moody. Ancient Apache–Navajo lands and lore link their tales.

Sergeant Charles Moody was thirty-two years old, a thirteen-year veteran of the United States Air Force with a high-security clearance at Holloman Air Force Base, in Alamogordo, New Mexico. He had logged over seven hundred hours as a flight mechanic on cargo planes, and an equal amount of time flying private aircraft.

In his words: "I have never seen any type of UFO in the past, or really cared much about them, except to crack a joke about, or make fun of, someone who claimed to have seen a UFO. I have never had any type of mental problems. I do not drink, only maybe a beer or two once in a while, never hard stuff. My health is very good. My eyesight is the best, twenty-twenty."

He was married, with two children, and had a nice home in Alamogordo. His wife, Karon, had ten years of experience as a nurse.

On the night of August 12, 1975, Moody finished his work shift at the air base at about eleven-thirty. He had heard that a meteor shower would be visible over the desert area at about one o'clock in the morning. If he was not too tired, he decided, he'd go out and have a look.

He drove home, changed clothes, watched television until about twelve-thirty, and was still feeling pretty wide awake. So he got into his car and drove a short way to a dirt road just outside Alamogordo at the edge of the White Sands Missile Range. He parked off the road, got out, and sat up on the left front fender of his car.

The night was clear, with a deep black sky full of glistening stars. Moody's expectations were not disappointed. For the next forty-five minutes, he watched eight or nine bright meteors streak across the open sky. But at about one-thirty he saw something that he had not expected to see.

"I observed a dull metallic object that seemed to just drop out of the sky and start to hover with a wobbling motion approximately one hundred feet in front of me, and approximately ten to fifteen feet off the ground. I was very frightened. The object was moving slowly toward my car. I jumped off the fender and got into my car. I tried to start it, but it was like there was no battery at all—the dome light and courtesy lights did not even come on when I opened the door. I couldn't understand that, because I keep my car in top-notch condition."

So Moody sat frozen, unable to flee, and scarcely understanding what was happening to him.

"At this time the object stopped dead still. It just hung in the air. The wobbling motion had stopped. It was dead still, about seventy to eighty feet away, and still fifteen to twenty feet off the ground."

It was a glowing saucer, about fifty feet in diameter, and approximately twenty feet from top to bottom. Moody was near panic.

"At this time, I heard a high-pitched sound, something like a dental drill might make at high speed. Then, just to the right center of the object, I saw what seemed to be an oblong-shaped window. I had not seen this before. It was approximately four to five feet long and two to three feet wide. At the window there were the shadows of what looked to be human forms. I could not make them out, only they looked humanoid. There were two or three of them at the window. Then the high-pitched sound stopped. A feeling of numbness came over my body. The fear that I had before left me. I felt a very peaceful, calm feeling come over my body. It was like floating on a cloud."

The next thing Moody knew, "the object lifted very fast and was gone. It made no sound as it left. Only it had a slight bit more glow than before. Then it was just gone. And after the object left, my car started perfectly."

Moody took off. He thought the entire sighting had lasted no more than a minute or two. But when he glanced at his watch, he received another jolt. It was two-forty-five in the morning. Just a moment or so before, he was sure, he had looked at his watch and it was only one-twenty.

When he got home, he told his wife what he had seen. He looked quite pale and sick to her. It was three o'clock by the wall clock. Moody said nothing to his wife about the missing time. He had a sense of needing medical help, but he was afraid to go to the military doctors.

Seeking some explanation of what had happened to him, he wrote a confidential letter to *Official UFO Magazine*. Stating that he feared for his job if any of his story was revealed, he nonetheless asked:

If you know of anyone who is knowledgeable about UFOs, and what could have possibly made me lose track of the time, would you please forward my letter to them and ask that it be kept confidential at this time? I would thank you very much for any help that you may give me.

I can tell you that I am sort of shook up over the fact that I lost that time, and I do not know what happened, if anything. I do not use any type of drug, nor had I been drinking at the time. Today is the day after the sighting. I feel great, only my back hurts a bit, and I feel a little light-headed. I do not know who to turn to for help or understanding. What I saw I only hope that you can help [me understand]. I am willing to talk with anyone who has an open mind and who is willing to keep my name confidential at this time.

Moody asked that he be contacted only at his home, definitely not at the air base. His request was forwarded to Jim Lorenzen, who finally reached Moody on August 21. By then, Moody said, something like a heat rash had broken out over his lower body, and his back was in considerable pain, as if "someone had hit him with a baseball bat."

He was scared, and he was going to turn himself in to sick call for treatment. But he could not tell the air force doctors what had happened, because he was afraid of what they might do in reaction.

Lorenzen told him, "The first thing they'll do is ship you out."

On September 2, Lorenzen and APRO field investigator W. C. Stevens flew to Alamogordo and met Sergeant Moody. An examination of the sighting area produced no evidence that a UFO had ever been there. But Moody himself seemed to undergo a strange transformation at the place.

According to Lorenzen, "When questioned at the site, Moody became quite agitated and admitted to feelings of apprehension and fear. These feelings were not nearly so pronounced when he was questioned away from the site, he [Moody] said. Several times during the Alamogordo interview, Chuck pointed out that he had had commando training and was not afraid of any man. But when probing questions were directed at him concerning the incident, he felt an urge to run away from the questioners [Mr. Stevens and me]. Moody also confessed to being very embarrassed by the fact that, previous to his experience, he had been the first to ridicule anybody who claimed to have seen a flying saucer. . . ."

After investigating Moody's background, family, home life, and reputation, Lorenzen concluded: "Our impression of Chuck Moody was that he was a responsible and conscientious person who had experienced something that he could not relate to previously held concepts, and he found that fact very unsettling."

Unfortunately, Moody seemed unable to remember anything that had occurred during his missing one hour and twenty-five minutes. The case, therefore, was interesting, but too sketchy to be considered of large significance.

Lorenzen advised Moody not to talk about the experience and never to call APRO from a base telephone, only from a "safe" phone outside the base. Moody, however, neglected the advice and called Lorenzen several times from the base. In one call, he reported that he had heard from "an old fishing buddy," Dr. Abraham Goldman, an ex-flight surgeon who had become a consultant in private neurosurgery practice.

Moody told Goldman his story. Goldman instructed him in self-hypnosis as a means of restoring the "lost memory" of the experience. It seemed to work. Moody began to remember further details, but he was stopped by a recalled suggestion that he would not remember anymore until some time had passed.

Meanwhile, he told Lorenzen, he had suddenly been ordered overseas. The transfer was effective immediately. But he refused to go before he could make provisions for his family to go with him. His transfer was extended to November 29.

On October 6, he again called Lorenzen and reported that he could remember what had happened—he had been on a spacecraft. Even so, his recall was considerably less than total. So plans were made for him to undergo regressive hypnosis in early November, before he had to go overseas.

Abruptly, Moody's transfer date was again changed, this time to October 29.

Still, the significance of his story did not loom large, especially in contrast to the Travis Walton case, which broke in early November. After Travis' return, APRO and the Lorenzens concentrated almost totally on the alleged abduction of the Snowflake wood-cutter.

Mail piled up at APRO's headquarters in Tucson. Not until November 15 did Lorenzen finally have a chance to go through it. Therein he discovered a letter from Moody, apparently written while Travis Walton was still missing, and certainly before anyone in the outside world had been told exactly what Travis claimed had happened to him.

Moody's letter read:

My dear friends Jim and Coral,

What I saw that night aboard their craft were things I cannot explain, but I can only try. The beings were about five-feet tall and very much like us, except their heads were larger and had no hair. Their eyes were larger than ours, ears very small, nose small, and the mouth had very thin lips. I would say their weight was maybe between one hundred ten and one hundred thirty pounds. There was speech, but their lips did not move. Their type of clothing was skin-tight. I could not see any zippers or buttons on their clothing at all. The color of their clothes was black, except for one of them, who had on a silver-white-looking suit.

There were no names said, but they knew who I was and called me by my proper name, Charles, and did not use my nickname, Chuck. It was like they could read my mind, and I believe that they did, because the elder, or leader, would speak sometimes before I would ask something.

I was taken to a room and the elder, or leader, touched my back and legs with a rod-like device. When I asked what he was doing, he said there had been a scuffle when they first made contact with me, and he only wanted to correct any misplacement that might have happened. I do not remember any type of scuffle or fight, but I do know my back hurt the next day.

The inside of the craft was as clean as an operating room. I cannot say if the fixtures were metal or plastic. The lighting was indirect. I did not see any source of light, but there was light. I was thinking to myself, *If I could only see the drive unit of the craft, how wonderful that would be*. The elder, or leader, put his hand on my shoulder and said to follow him.

We went to a small room that had no fixtures in it and which was dimly lit, and [we] stood on the side of the room. The floor seemed to give way, like an elevator. I guess we went down about six feet, and what I saw then was a room about twenty-five feet across. In the center was what looked like a huge carbon rod going through the roof of the room; around the rod were three of what looked like holes covered with glass. Inside the glass-covered holes or balls were what looked like large crystals with two rods, one on each side of the crystal. One rod came to a ball-like top; the other one came to a T-type top. I was told that this was the drive unit, and that I could understand it if I tried. There were no wires or cables. I then saw what looked like a large black box on one side of the room. I asked about it and was told what it was, but then I was told not to ever reveal what the black box was for. I have really tried to remember, but I can't remember about the black box, only that it was there.

I guess I was there about half an hour looking at the drive unit. I was then taken back up through the same way we had come down. That part of the floor just went up with us. The elder, or leader, then told me that this was not their main craft, but [was one] used only for observing, and that their main craft was about four hundred of our miles above the earth. And the drive unit on it was different from the one on this craft. I asked if I could go to the main craft, and—I was told no, that their time was short, but they could find me any time they desired, and that in a short time they would see me again.

I then asked the leader, or elder, why was I so sluggish and clumsy, and he told me that I was quite hostile at the first contact and that they had to use a type of sound or light on me to calm me down, and that the effect would go away in a short time. The elder, or leader, then put both his hands on the sides of my head and told me it was time for them to leave, and he asked me not to remember what had been said, or what I had seen, for at least two weeks. I don't know why the two weeks, but I guess there was a reason, because it was about two weeks later that [Jim Lorenzen] came to Alamogordo, and shortly after that it started coming back to me —what had happened to me.

I asked him [the elder] if we would meet again, and he said yes, in a short time. And he then told me to be sure and visit a doctor soon. . . . I then asked why they had talked to me, and why was I taken on board their craft. He said only that in time "you will understand."

The next thing I knew, I was sitting in my car, watching a strange object lift into the sky and trying to start my car. . . .

Four days later, a sequence of UFO sightings in and around the Navajo–Hopi Indian reservation area began with the sudden loss of total power in a Ford Bronco police patrol van near Keams Canyon.

Less than three months later, the Travis Walton saga began—certainly the most astounding in a series of startling events that had confounded the Mogollon skies, both before and after the alleged Walton abduction.

But what, if anything, did it all mean?

Chuck Moody offered his answer, even as Duane Walton was voicing similar ideas during the search for his brother in the Turkey Springs woods.

Said Moody, "The people of this world have really misunderstood UFOers and what they are doing. It's not only just one advanced race that is studying this planet earth, but a group of them, and within three years from now they will make themselves known to all mankind. It may be as early as mid-summer 1976. I can also say that it will not be a pleasant type of meeting, for there will be warnings made to the people of this world. Their plan is for only limited contact, and after twenty years of further study and only after deeper consideration will there be any type of closer contact.

"They also fear for their own lives and will protect themselves at all costs. Their intent is a peaceful one, and if the leaders of this world will only heed their warnings, we will find ourseves a lot better off than before. And at this time, it's not up to us to accept them, but for them to accept us . . . !"

10.

WITH THE FALLING SNOWS OF THE NEW YEAR, A FRAGILE quietude settled down on the wintry Mogollon Plateau. The Travis Walton case seemed to be dormant. The reporters were gone; the UFO "experts" were gone. Frenzy appeared to have slipped away from the frontier towns, leaving the citizens at peace again.

Officially, Sheriff Gillespie closed the case: he couldn't prove that Travis had been abducted by an alien spacecraft; he couldn't disprove it. The press had portrayed him as a disbeliever. Some of his friends knew better. He had privately confided that the Walton story, in some respects, was believable—improbably, but still feasible. The evidence was inconclusive. However, the sheriff had other work to do. He couldn't spend his whole life chasing the ghosts flitting around the Travis Walton case. But some of his deputies quietly continued the pursuit, as did the UFO investigating organizations, whose pursuit was not always so quiet. Thus, if the controversy no longer raged worldwide, it did smolder, and it occasionally flared up hotly— mainly within the burbling caldrons of UFologist journals, whose reports were sometimes briefly quoted in the public prints, usually the hot stuff.

Skylook, the official publication of the Mutual UFO Network, early reported:

> Under-sheriff Kenneth Coplan noted . . . that Walton and the other forestry workers had seen the October 20 NBC special, "The UFO Incident," which described Betty and Barney Hill being taken

aboard a UFO, and [he] suggested that some aspects of the two cases were similar.

The veiled implication was that the Walton abduction had been copied from the TV show, which depicted the decade-old Hill story. A biracial New Hampshire couple, the Hills claimed to have been intercepted on a lonely mountain road, and they "woke up" sometime later, and miles away from where they had been. The Hills eventually recalled being examined by strange creatures aboard a spaceship.

Skylook, however, did not report the forestry workers' reaction to the claim that they had watched the Hill special.

Travis Walton denied that he had seen the show. "I didn't even have a television set," he said.

Mike Rogers said, "I did watch the first part of it. But then I turned it off because it was boring. I just was not all that interested in UFOs before this thing happened."

The rest of the crew, when questioned, either did not remember if they had watched the show, or else they denied seeing it. In either case, the entire crew steadfastly maintained that they saw what they saw in the woods—and it had nothing to do with a television show or anything else that they knew about.

The UFO Investigator, NICAP's publication, reported:

> As with all contactee cases, the alleged abduction of a twenty-two-year-old forestry service crew member has created undue excitement and interest throughout the country.

NICAP stated that, based on its reports, the "facts naturally throw the case under great suspicion, and it would seem that either a hoax has been committed or that a psychological phenomena [sic] is involved."

NICAP's "facts" were that its investigator, Dr. William S. Bickel, professor of physics at the University of Arizona questioned the polygraph tests given to the Rogers' crew. He claimed that the tests had been given in three parts:

1). *Was any witness involved with foul play or angry at Travis Walton?*

2). *Did any witness know if anyone else was involved with foul play?*

3). *What did each witness see?*

Bickel said that truthful answers to #1 and #2 would constitute "passing the lie-detector test," even if #3 was answered falsely, and #3 was the only relevant question.

In addition, NICAP reported that Sheriff Gillespie had claimed that Travis had telephoned a radio talk show before the abduction and had volunteered to appear as a guest. The talk-show host called Walton a "kook."

After Travis "returned," he called the talk show again and said, "Who's a kook now?"

NICAP also repeated the unsubstantiated assertion that Travis Walton had long been an avid UFO buff.

It was apparent, however, that NICAP's "facts" were badly jumbled. Bickel's alleged assessment of the polygraph tests indicated that he did not know exactly what questions had been asked, and he did not know how such tests were graded.

Number 3, *What did each witness see?*, could not possibly be asked on any polygraph exam, since all questions had to be phrased to elicit only a "yes" or "no" answer.

Further, all questions had to be answered truthfully, not just two out of three, in order for a "passing grade" to be given.

Polygraph examiner Gilson had asked specific questions of the Rogers' men, and all of them answered all of the questions truthfully, except Allen Dalis, whose test was marked inconclusive.

When questioned, Bickel admitted that he had not conducted any formal investigation of the Walton case. Instead, he had written two letters to NICAP, based on what he had read in the newspapers, and addended by what Deputy Coplan had told him.

Therefore, the sheriff's department was asked for its corroboration of the talk-show story. What station was it on? Who was the host?

Under-sheriff Romo replied that the whole story was "a bunch of malarkey, a rumor—it never happened."

And Coplan said that Bickel was wrong—he never told such a story to Bickel, or anyone else.

Bickel finally admitted that he had no evidence whatever that Travis Walton was an avid UFO buff.

Thus, the main "facts" supporting NICAP's damning conclusion were all false.

Whereupon, *Skylook* commented on the entire affair and fell right back into the same rumor-ridden rut: NICAP's report had not been based on a "thorough job," but in the future "positive and/or negative data would be published in follow-up articles. Apparently NICAP has knowledge that Travis Walton's mother is an avid UFO buff who has, in the past, expressed a desire for personal UFO abduction."

To which "fact" *Skylook* added smugly: "Perhaps if the whole family had been taken, we would not be mixed up in this confusing case, intermixed with conflicting organizations, personalities, undocumented statements, *etc.*"

Most of the conflict and confusion, however, was not the fault of the family. It was the fault of the organizations themselves, competing against each other, confounding the case with their own disquiet personalities, and relying for evidence upon undocumented news reports and unsubstantiated statements from their own investigators, as well as from several police officers.

Reports said that "troopers present" heard Mary Walton Kellet make suspicious statements when she was informed that her son was missing.

However, Mike Rogers replied, "There was only one 'trooper' present, Ken Coplan. And she did not make the 'suspicious' statements attributed to her by him."

Coplan acknowledged that she had not; she had only acted unsurprised that her son had been taken.

Spaulding's own report was a classic, characterized by its error and illogic. In *Skylook*'s roundup of investigative analyses, it was quoted thusly:

GSW Evaluation:

After a time-consuming investigation, the Travis Walton case is considered a hoax based on the following:

1). Walton never boarded the UFO. This fact is supported by the six witnesses and the polygraph [Gilson] test results.

2). The entire Walton family has had a continual UFO history. The Walton boys have reported observing ten to fifteen separate UFO sightings [very high].

3). When Duane was questioned about his brother's disappearance, he stated that "Travis will be found," that "UFO's are friendly."

GSW countered, "How do you know that Travis will be found?"

Duane said, "I have a feeling, a strong feeling."

GSW asked, "If the UFO captors are going to return Travis, will you have a camera to record this great occurrence?"

Duane said, "No. If I have a camera, *they* will not return."

4). The Waltons' mother showed no outward emotion over the "loss" of Travis. She said that UFOs would not harm her son, that he would be returned, and that UFOs had been seen by her family many times.

5). The Waltons refused any outside scientific help or anyone who logically doubted the abduction portion of the story.

6). The media and GSW were fair to the witnesses. However, when the story started to fall apart, the Waltons would talk only to people who did not doubt the abduction story.

7). The Waltons sold their story to the *National Enquirer,* and the story was completely twisted from the truth.

The polygraph tests administered to the Rogers' crew did not support the "fact" that "Walton never boarded the UFO." Spaulding had no evidence supporting his premise that Walton did not go aboard. Conversely, the tests tended to support the witnesses' claim that "that's where he must be, aboard the UFO." Spaulding himself believed that the crew had, indeed, encountered a UFO.

His summary of "evidence" falsely stated that the entire family had an obsessive UFO history, that the Waltons refused any outside scientific help, that the media and GSW had been fair in the case, that the story had started to fall apart, and that the *National Enquirer* story was completely twisted from the truth.

The *Enquirer* story was basically correct in its details,

but it had failed to mention the McCarthy polygraph test, which Walton flunked, but which Spaulding did not even know about.

According to Spaulding, "He [Travis] has never taken a polygraph test!"

Some of the statements attributed to Duane and his mother were only partially correct. Duane especially had made some wild statements to a lot of people during his brother's disappearance—to ease his mother's fears, he claimed. And he himself was all hyped up at the time, not an unusual reaction for a man whose brother had allegedly been spirited away by alien space creatures. The Waltons, after all, were only human, and not superhumanly possessed of invincible reason or unflappable aplomb. Had they been conspiring in a hoax, in fact, their "suspicious" behavior and statements probably would have been tailored otherwise. Instead, they acted very much like themselves, suddenly thrust into just such a bizarre experience—which, of course, was not in itself iron-clad proof of their innocence.

An especially glaring falsehood in the Spaulding evaluation was the charge that the Waltons had refused scientific testing. In fact, they had done exactly the opposite. They had sought and submitted to every form of testing available to them—except when agreements attached to certain tests were abrogated by the would-be testers.

In sum, exactly none of Spaulding's "evidence" factually supported his shotgun conclusion that the Travis Walton case was a hoax. For all anyone could prove at the time, it might have been a hoax. But the cold, clinical, objective fact was that no evidence had been developed to either prove or disprove the story. The illogical, convoluted, error-filled reports of the experts proved nothing. But they revealed a good deal about the experts themselves, while they further distorted the already baffling case.

And the distortions then heaped further discredit upon the Walton story, in the public eye, jaundicing the public's view of the entire episode: the Waltons were not credible people; therefore, their story was a hoax.

Even APRO—the most professionally adept of the bickering UFO investigating agencies—was not immune to reporting error in its bulletins. But APRO's errors were both few and slight. And its competent staff had both the good sense and the selfless grace to correct its errors in follow-up reports.

There was, perhaps happily, even a vein of unintended humor stricken through the confusing lode of material mined up by the scrambling and dispeptically eclectic experts.

One British publication, the *Flying Saucer Review,* deadpanned (with a monocle implanted firmly over an arched eye): "Is Duane Smith [of the Rogers crew] Travis' brother?" Heh?

To which Travis sent the equally arch reply: *"Dwayne Smith is not my brother, but Duane Walton is."* Harummmph!

And sniggers of laughter made the rounds of Snowflake when its leading John Bircher, Vance Rogers, also the town barber, unequivocally announced that he believed the Walton story completely.

Responded Glen Flake: "Vance believes this story all the way . . . but he probably doesn't believe that we put a man on the moon. That, he'd say, was done in Hollywood to fool the people of the country into believing that their tax money was being well spent, instead of squandered on liberal left-wing lunacies."

Snowflake schoolchildren composed scornful ditties about the abduction. Graffiti covered some walls in the town. One story making the rounds told of two men who met on Main Street.

"Hey," one says, "did you hear that they found out Travis Walton was telling the truth?"

"Really?"

"Yeah. They found a Mars Bar in his pocket."

Still, levity was not a hallmark of the time and events. Unfortunately, many lives were torn apart and twisted in the churning aftermath. Families were split in their beliefs. Even the Mormon religion was strongly tested by it all. Rash things were said and done by many people, renting the harmony that had taken a century of small-town co-existence to knit together. Snowflake had never been so sundered before. But it was not always an open division, outspoken and up front. Rather, it was quiet and subtle, all the more invidious for its sly invisibility—the slick needle, rather than the broad sword. It didn't kill; it only maimed—and not the body, just the heart. The most obvious victims were the main characters themselves and their families.

Mike Rogers was accused of participating in a hoax to get out of his behind-schedule work contract. Forest Service Contracting Officer Maurice Marchbanks called such accusations nonsense; there was no way such an alleged hoax could benefit Rogers.

Mike's immediate Forest Service supervisor, Junior Williams, added: "He had no reason . . . I didn't see that he had anything to gain, as far as his contract was concerned, or anything else, to conjure up a story of this kind. He did lose the contract later on, because he couldn't get men to go back and work for him in that area. We did readvertise the contract and resell it to another person."

Mike was paid for the work his crew had done, and his successor finished the job at approximately the same time that Rogers would have completed the contract had there been no UFO disruption.

Mike was also a husband and a father, an intelligent man, one who had been known for his quiet strength, an equable man of gentle passions. But his changed life changed him by almost imperceptible degrees. Since he was a very accomplished and natural artist, he firstly reacted through his art. He painted a large-canvas, photo-realistic portrait of the saucer firing its beam into Travis Walton, with Walton just being flung backward over a log.

Mike explained what he had done. "Working from the composite descriptions of all of us, I have painted a detailed scene of what we all saw that fifth day of November when Travis was hit by the beam emitted from the UFO. The reason I did the painting is because so many people say we don't know what we saw, or say we were tricked, or say there was a hoax. I know as sure as I breathe that was in no way a ball of gas, or dust, or some kind of illusion. My eyesight has always been extremely keen, and I know exactly what I saw.

"Even as detailed as I did the painting, it does not compare to the beauty and perfection of the object we all saw that night. The picture isn't exactly quite right. And all the guys say, yeah, that's very close, but there's something about it that isn't quite right, and I can't exactly say what it is. Nobody can explain what it is. There was something indefinable about the object itself, this grandeur it had, the feeling it gave us to look at it. And the sound it made is something else that we can't really explain. It was so powerful, and it had so many tones sounding simultaneously.

"Anymore, when people make these ridiculous accusations against us, I feel like fighting—it makes me that mad. I wish they could have been there to see what we saw. The awesomeness of the UFO was something that could not be faked. And that's what people are refusing to grasp—what all of us saw, even before Travis was struck by the beam. The best I can do now is to show them my painting."

But that wasn't enough. And as time and controversy wore on, Mike described the growing effects of the experience on his life. "There is an attitude that you feel from other people. They don't actually say anything. But at the store checkout, or on the street, or in a restaurant . . . they look at you, and you don't know what they're thinking. But it is different from the way they were before this happened.

"My wife, Katie, was near a mental breakdown. [She protests the terminology and suggests 'deep shock' is closer to what she was undergoing.] It's changed our lives. I can't get a job, for one thing. Maybe people think I'm going to disrupt the other workers, or they don't believe the story so they don't trust me, or something like that. The reason doesn't matter so much. What matters is that I'm broke, I have no prospects for work, I'm behind on the rent, they're ready to shut off the electricity, I have kids to feed, and I don't know what to do about it."

Once, Katie literally fled from the house, seeking haven with Travis' mother. "I wish he would do something, anything," Katie pleaded. "It's very hard, what's happening to us. He sits around the house all day. There's no money coming in. We start to fight. I'm over here now because he told me to go out, get out. I have to get away from him; he gets so moody."

Mary understood completely. She had been hurt as badly as anyone in the aftermath of the event. But more was yet to come: charge and counter-charge; action and reaction. Not till a full year later could any of the people involved accurately gauge the complete impact of the cause-and-effect vortex into which their lives had been dumped.

Allen Dalis went to jail.

Ken Peterson fled to Mexico.

Steve Pierce was tempted by a Judas role.

Travis complained of suffering from horrendous nightmares. He fought back against his attackers by letter, on radio, on television; he even took to lecturing on a ministump of college campuses. At least he made a living with appearance fees—a lot less than what he had been making at his job, he claimed.

He was not unaware of the scorn and contempt in which he was held by some of his fellow townsmen. And he grated under the ridicule flung at him from more distant accusers. He was prideful, his ego was not small, and defense of himself became his life, consuming him. This, after all, was how people were going to think of him forever after. Everything that he might ever do, or try to become, would always be controlled, not by his own will and his own efforts, but by what other people said about his "abduction" by a UFO.

And people were saying that he was a liar, a hoaxer, a fraud. Look at his record! He was a criminal, wasn't he?

Rue Hendrickson was the owner of the Cedar Motel—tax and accounting services also available. He was a tall, lean, drawling country man with a sharp eye, good sense, and a sound heart that was not slow to offer a helping hand when it was needed.

"He went off on a ride in a flying saucer? I don't believe it," Rue said. "Bullshit! Long before this happened, I thought he and Duane were big bullshitters. They exaggerated everything. I don't trust them as far as I can throw them. But they sure got a lot of publicity out of this. Maybe that's what it was all about. Everybody in the world knows about Snowflake now, knows where it is. That's the place where that guy got kidnapped by a UFO. Bullshit! I don't believe it.

"But all those other six guys are sincere in what they say. They passed the polygraph test. The witnesses all tell the same story. They sincerely believe it, and I believe them. They saw something. But what did they see?"

Marshal Sank Flake had already given his answer. But, he admitted, "A lot of people believe it happened.

My sister believes every word of it. My brother Glen believes it, though he's had some doubts. My father doesn't buy any of it. I don't think there's any real trouble about it—some folks just have differing views. The only real trouble seems to be between the Waltons and Sank Flake, because I spoke out about what I thought. I thought it was a hoax, and I said so. I talked to Travis for a good long time about it, and we're not so angry with each other anymore. He told me, 'It's a fact. It happened just like I said it did. I wasn't lying.' He acts like that's the truth. Some people believe it. Some don't. And some just plain don't care one way or the other."

Sank, like several other lawmen, questioned the validity of the polygraph test given by Cy Gilson to the six witnesses. How good was it? How specific and complete were the questions concerning the UFO?

Glen Flake lived just one house away from his brother on Stinson Street, a block off Main Street. Glen's house was a big, roomy, comfortable rancher, full of deep-sitting, homey furniture. Burning logs crackled in the fireplace. The grown-up kids sprawled on chairs and sofas, while the grandkids lay quietly on Indian rugs spread across the hardwood floors. The children listened attentively to a family discussion until, one by one, they finally rolled over and fell into untroubled sleep.

The discussion was about the Travis Walton story. Ruminating about it now, a year later, Glen said, "I discount a lot of the story because I know Travis. I discount a lot of it more because of Travis than anything else. I just don't put much faith in him. The other boys, yes, I have faith in them. I've known Ken Peterson and Mike Rogers all their lives. They are truthful and good boys. They wouldn't lie to me, though they might have been fooled, too.

"And I have faith in the lie-detector test. According to him [Gilson], those boys weren't lying about seeing a UFO. Out at the search, I had to believe what they were saying, that Travis must have gone off on the UFO. But then, the way it all ended up, I began to have my doubts. Travis mysteriously reappears. The sheriff wasn't notified that he was back. We got a tip that he had made a phone call from Heber, and I went over to the mother's house, and he was in there. But the family didn't tell me that he was back.

"They called the sheriff's office for help when he disappeared, but then they didn't tell the sheriff when he came back. They were hiding him out. But it is possible that Duane thought they could make some money out of it. It would be just like Duane: here comes Travis back and Duane says, let's hide him, until Duane can figure out how best to make some money out of it.

"And it just looked strange that it should suddenly happen to that family, what with all the problems that they've had since they've been here, especially Travis."

Oh, yeah, the older kids laughed. Travis was wild in his teen-age days, always into something, mainly just prankish jokes, really, nothing real harmful or serious. But Kenny—they weren't all that sure about Glen's high estimation of Kenny Peterson.

"Why not?" he asked.

"Because," his oldest son answered, "Kenny took off for Mexico, got married down there, and then took up with that new religion."

He rolled his eyes with mock alarm, scoffing at Kenny's supposed abdication from strict Mormonism. The others laughed, realizing that he was only fooling.

"Kenny's just a little mixed up," Glen's daughter Debby said. "I think it all just confused him, so he ran away from it. Something about the UFO and the religion bothered him. But there's no real conflict. It's in the Scriptures: there will be signs in the skies. The signs could be UFOs. We believe that there is life on other planets. But it is life like us, all made by God. All the people, wherever they are, are made in His image and likeness. So I don't like Travis' story about the three creatures. I don't like that, and I don't believe it."

The others are no longer laughing. Debby is quite serious. Mormon beliefs are serious to all of them.

Very gently, Glen said, "But the three other people were just like us. What he described were people just like us. And, remember, we used to send our spacecraft up with monkeys in them. The monkeys weren't human, but they were on our spacecraft. So think about that."

The others nodded, yes, that's true. Something very

much like that could very well explain the existence of Travis' three hairless fetal dwarfs.

Then someone suggested that Travis' three idealized humans might have originated in the mind of his fundamental Mormon beliefs—made ideally in the image and likeness of God. This would fit exactly with what the psychiatrists said: Travis might have suffered a temporary psychosis and his mind imagined what he thought was happening.

Well, all that psychiatric mumbo-jumbo, you know (they all agreed), it's a lot of guessing, and maybes, and it never proves anything.

"To tell the truth," Mrs. Flake said, "I'd love to believe Travis' story. It's so exciting. But I wouldn't like being fooled—I'd hate to say I believe it, and then it turns out to be a hoax. I just don't trust Travis. That's the main reason that I don't believe the story."

Yes, her family nodded in unison, Travis himself is the factor that gives pause to his own story.

"But," Mrs. Flake said, "the things that people were saying about his mother weren't true. I know that. I know that she was not in on it, if it was a hoax. And I doubt very much that Travis, or any of the others, would be able to pull the wool over her eyes—about this or anything else. She's too smart.

"And I have to admit that the boys . . . all of them certainly seem to have changed. They've all matured, cleaned themselves up. I even saw Travis at Sunday school. They are like different people now, sincere and humble. But maybe that is all just to get people to believe them."

"Could be that the experience has changed them," her older son suggested.

"Could be," she replied. "But I still wouldn't like getting caught believing it, if it does turn out to be a hoax."

"I guess I really believed the story," Glen said. "Then time went on and I didn't believe it. Now, when I think about it all over again, I tend to believe it again. Considering all the fors and againsts, I tend to think it happened, just like the boys said it did. I can't disbelieve it just because it's Travis. There are too many other factors involved, and they seem to support the story.

"For one thing, there are the lights. We have all seen

them. Maybe we don't know what they are, but we have seen them. A lot of people have seen them. So you can't really discount the Walton story just because the Waltons have seen the same lights that everybody else has seen. Whatever those lights are, they are not normal.

"Maybe Sank doesn't believe that they exist. Maybe some people are angry because they think the religion is being blasphemed. And it certainly is peculiar the way this happened; it's peculiar that it happened to them, the Waltons. That just makes it look suspicious to a lot of people.

"I guess, finally, I don't believe it, and I don't disbelieve it. I just don't know what the truth of it is. Maybe we'll never know. . . ."

11.

AS A LEGITIMATE AND RESPECTED RESEARCH ORGANIZA-
tion, APRO's effectiveness depended upon its credibility.
It enjoyed a worldwide reputation for doing deliberative,
thorough, scientific investigations of alleged UFO incidents. And its competence was acknowledged even outside
the field of UFology itself.

So the last thing it needed was to be caught defending
a hoax. Thereby, all that it had stood for would be lost.
Yet, APRO certainly seemed to be inching out on the
proverbial limb with the Travis Walton case. Sometimes,
APRO seemed to be its sole defender.

In explanation of its role, Director Jim Lorenzen wrote:
"The consulting and administrative staffs of APRO feel
that the Travis Walton case is one of the most important
and intriguing in the history of the UFO phenomena; and
that it demands a clarification of any inaccuracies that may
creep in during the process of relating information from
witness to researcher."

APRO, of course, knew about the secret McCarthy
polygraph test, which Travis had failed. The failed test,
regardless of extenuating circumstances, was a flaw in the
case. No scientific study could possibly ignore that flaw.
Therefore, the test would have to be given again. Without
retesting, the entire scientific procedure would be in question, its final results flawed.

Preliminary arrangements were made with the Ezell
Polygraph Institute of Phoenix. But there were complica-
tions. APRO wanted to test both Duane and Travis. In
addition, it wanted several of its scientific consultants

present: psychologist Dr. Leo Sprinkle, chief of the University of Wyoming's testing and counseling department, and physiologist-parapsychologist Dr. Harold Cahn. Dr. Sprinkle, for one, could not participate before February 7, so that date was finally chosen.

Lorenzen made an appointment with Tom Ezell to test only Duane that day. Travis, he later said, had been having trouble with his car, and it was a long drive from Snowflake; since his arrival time was indefinite, no appointment was made for him.

On February 6, Lorenzen called Ezell to confirm the test time, one P.M. Saturday. Ezell asked if his associate, George Pfeifer, could conduct the test.

"What is his competence?" Lorenzen asked.

"He's as qualified as I am," Ezell answered. "He's an ex-policeman, with a lot of experience in law enforcement. He's up on all the latest methods."

Lorenzen agreed to the change.

On Saturday, Drs. Sprinkle and Cahn, with APRO's Jim Lorenzen and Hal Starr, met with Pfeifer to determine what Duane would be asked. Dr. Sprinkle had prepared a set of possible questions. Pfeifer made some changes, the test was reviewed with Duane, and he entered the examination room with Pfeifer.

Then, according to APRO, Travis arrived from Snowflake with some friends, and he asked if he could be tested as soon as Duane was finished. That was fine with APRO, if Pfeifer had the time. The APRO team then began discussing the material to be covered in Travis' test, while Travis and his friends took a walk in the park across the street.

Pfeifer's report describes Duane's test:

The purpose of this examination was to determine the accuracy of his statements regarding incidents involving a UFO experience on November 5, 1975, through the morning of November 11.

Prior to the examination, all questions were reviewed with Duane Walton. He was given opportunities to reject and/or accept any and all questions. He was at liberty to change the phraseology of questions or develop his own questions.

After completion of the question formulation, all

tests were again reviewed with him. He agreed to answer all and signed the consent waiver form. This test was performed using a Lafayette Polygraph Model #76056-B.

Initially, a "known lie test" was developed. This was through the use of playing cards. It was determined that Duane Walton was a strong responder, and was suitable for a polygraph examination.

The test formulation used was the relevant/irrelevant type of question structure. The relevant questions used were:

Test 1

4). Were you in contact with Travis between 11-6-75 and 11-10-75?—"No."

6). Would you lie to help Travis in this matter?—"No."

7). Did Travis hide on the Kellett ranch?—"No."

9). Do you always tell the truth in matters of major importance?—"Yes."

10). Did you spend approximately one and one-quarter hours in Lester Steward's office?—"Yes."

11). Is Travis normally clean-shaven?—"Yes."

Test 2

1). Were you aware that Travis was missing before you received the telephone call from your mother?—"No."

2). Did you participate in a hoax to pretend that Travis was missing?—"No."

3). Do you believe that Travis participated in a hoax to pretend that he was missing?—"No."

4). Do you know where Travis was located during the several days while he was missing?—"No."

5). Do you believe that Travis is sincere in describing his experience while he was missing?—"Yes."

6). Are you telling me the truth now?—"Yes."

7). Were you and Travis in Lester Steward's office only once?—"Yes."

8). Prior to November 5, 1975, had you read a book on UFOs?—"No."

After a careful analysis of the polygrams produced, along with information gained during pre-test and post-test interviews, it is the opinion of this examiner that Duane Walton has answered all questions truthfully according to what he believes to be the truth regarding this incident, and he has not attempted to be deceptive in any area.

So Duane passed. But in doing so, he admitted spending considerably more time with Lester Steward than had previously been claimed, about fifty minutes. The significance seemed minimal. Steward himself had claimed that his "interrogation" of the Waltons had lasted for two hours.

More importantly, Pfeifer seemingly cleared Duane of participation in a hoax. Duane had "answered all questions truthfully."

Next was Travis. While reviewing his test with Pfeifer, Travis said that several accusations that had been made against him were not covered in the questions. He wanted questions designed so that he could directly answer the specific accusations.

Pfeifer's report describes the test:

Mr. Travis Walton was given a polygraph examination at this office at three P.M., February 7, 1976. The purpose of this examination was to determine the truth in his statements regarding a UFO incident that occurred on 11-5-75 and lasting until the early morning hours of 11-11-75, as reported by Travis. This examination was performed by using a Lafayette Polygraph Model #76056-B.

During a pre-test interview, it was determined that Travis Walton was well rested and cooperative, was feeling physically fit, and preliminary tests indicated he was a suitable subject for the examination.

A discussion was held and we mutually designed questions for this examination. Prior to the examination, all questions were again reviewed with him. He agreed to answer all and signed the consent waiver form. Question formulation was of the relevant/irrelevant type. Following is a list of the relevant questions used in this examination:

3). Are there approximately only two hours you recall during your experience?—"Yes."

4). Did you find yourself on a table inside a strange room?—"Yes."

6). Did you see strange-looking beings inside the strange room?—"Yes."

7). Have you been reasonably accurate in describing your experience?—"Yes."

9). Did you conspire with another to perpetrate a hoax about this matter?—"No."

10). Were you struck by a blue-green ray on the evening of 11-5-75?—"Yes."

11). Since November 1, 1975, have you used any illegal narcotic drugs?—"No."

13). Before November 5, 1975, were you a UFO buff?—"No."

14). Have you been completely truthful with Mr. Lorenzen in this matter?—"Yes."

15). Did you see a UFO on the evening of 11-5-75?—"Yes."

It should be noted that questions #9, 10, 11, 13, and 15 were used in this examination exactly as Mr. Travis Walton dictated them to this examiner. Mr. Walton was completely cooperative during this examination.

There was some slight response regarding question #10 (Were you struck by a blue-green ray?). After the first chart was run, it was determined that Travis had not actually seen a "blue-green ray" coming from the alleged UFO. He did see the area illuminated with a "greenish light."

After a careful analysis of the polygrams produced, there are no areas left unresolved, and it is the opinion of this examiner that Travis Walton has answered all questions in a manner that he himself is firmly convinced to be truthful regarding the incident commencing 11-5-75.

So Travis passed. Curiously enough, the question to which response was recorded, #10, had been "dictated" by Travis himself. The others specifically dealt with charges that he had conspired in a hoax, had been hallucinating on drugs, was an avid UFO buff, and did not actually see a UFO on the night of the alleged abduction.

Pfeifer did not specifically ask if Travis had committed a hoax by himself, without the help of others. And he did not ask if Travis had been hiding during the five days of his disappearance. But those questions seemingly were answered in response to the more general questions: Have you been reasonably accurate in describing your experience? Have you been completely truthful with Mr. Lorenzen in this matter? "Yes," Travis answered.

Oddly enough, Pfeifer did not report that Travis had answered all questions truthfully—as he had phrased it in Duane's report. Rather, Pfeifer's opinion was that "Travis Walton has answered all questions *in a manner that he himself is firmly convinced to be truthful. . . .*"

It was a small hole through which critics might drive huge trucks.

But, verbally, Pfeifer told APRO that both Duane and Travis had passed their tests. They were being truthful about the alleged UFO abduction and their respective roles in all that surrounded it.

All the main characters in the human drama had, thus, been polygraphed—except for one, Mary Walton Kellet. And she also had been accused of foul complicity in the alleged hoax. So she also submitted to a lie-detector test, administered by George Pfeifer.

His report stated:

Prior to the examination, in a pre-test interview, it was determined that she was not under any medication, did not have any cardiac conditions, and in general was in fit physical and mental condition to undergo the examination.

Prior to the examination, a "known lie test" was performed and her deceptive responses were determined. These were used as a guide on the main relevant test issues. Question formulation was the relevant/irrelevant type. A Stoelting Emotional Stress Monitor, Model #22600, was used.

All questions were reviewed with her. She agreed to answer all and signed the consent waiver form.

Following are listed the main relevant-issue questions and her answers:

Test 1

3). Did you ever conspire with Travis or any person to perpetrate a hoax to pretend that Travis was missing?—"No."

4). Were you deeply involved in the UFO subject before Travis' disappearance?—"No."

6). During the period of 11-6-75 to 11-10-75, did you actually know where Travis was?—"No."

7). Did you ever tell anyone during that period that you would not be surprised if he had been abducted by a flying saucer?—"No."

9). Have you at any time read a book about flying saucers?—"No."

10). Were you notified of Travis' disappearance by only two people, Mike Rogers and Ken Coplan, and no one else?—"Yes."

Test 2

1). Do you always tell the truth on matters of major importance?—"Yes."

2). Did you ever discuss flying saucers with Sheriff Gillespie before 11-5-75?—"No."

3). Have you on any occasion refused admittance to your home to Marshal Sanford Flake?—"No."

4). Would you lie to help Travis in this matter? —"No."

5). Did you conceal Travis from public contact between 11-5-75 and 11-11-75?—"No."

6). Do you believe that Travis is truthful in this matter?—"Yes."

7). Have you yourself ever seen a flying saucer? —"No."

After a very careful analysis of the polygrams produced, and comparing the polygram tracings with the Known Lie pattern, it is the opinion of this examiner that Mrs. Mary Walton Kellet has answered all the questions truthfully according to the best of her knowledge and beliefs.

And so Mary also passed. According to Pfeifer, she had answered truthfully all the accusations that had been made against her about a hoax, conspiracy, concealing Travis during his disappearance, and previous obsession with UFOs.

The problem was, she had also said that she had never seen a flying saucer. What she had seen were what other people called UFOs, and the niggling distinction is what the raging critics failed to make. To see a saucer is to see an object of definite framework and structure. To see a UFO is to see something less definite, though, theoretically, it may very well be a flying saucer...

The exact problem was that Mary had told people about the distant lights that she had seen. Ergo, in some minds, she was lying when she said she had never seen a flying saucer. From the splitting of such hairs, great fabrics of conflict were woven.

With the tests thus concluded, APRO's position seemed to be rooted on solid ground. And it noted: "In UFO research, circumstances require that many rumors and details must be pursued in order to develop a case fully. Tips and rumors, both positive and negative, must be developed to determine their merit. While this is time-consuming, there seems to be no alternative, for false rumors, if left unchecked, could distort the total picture. . . .

"Concern has been expressed in the UFO field concerning the diverse opinions and information developed by different organizations reporting on the case. Contributing to this situation has been the fact that certain law officers in the Holbrook, Snowflake, and Heber areas have promoted rumors that attack the character and motivations of the principals of the case. Apparently, this has been done partly because the incident embodies connotations that they personally do not want to face. On Sheriff Gillespie's part, political expediency certainly has to be considered as a factor. Since his office is elective, it should not surprise anyone to find him playing to the majority of his electorate, who would rather not believe that such ominous things as UFO kidnappings could occur in their community—this, in spite of the fact that he seems to be much more of a UFO buff than the Waltons. . . .

141

"A pattern emerges that suggests that many people involved in 'investigation' have been much more careless with the truth than the witnesses. All the principals involved in the experience of Travis Walton, including the six witnesses to the initial incident, have undergone testing via polygraph. It occurs [to APRO] that in order to close this case, the individuals whose testimony conflicts with that of Mrs. Kellet, Travis and Duane Walton, as well as the six individual witnesses, should volunteer, as the foregoing have, to submit to a polygraph test to determine their roles in the case. Those individuals include Sheriff Gillespie, Sanford Flake, Ken Coplan, Bill Spaulding, Lester Steward. . . . APRO will be happy to underwrite the cost of these tests, and only awaits the acquiescence of the participants. . . ."

None acquiesced.

By then, APRO disclosed its appraisal of the main character in the bewildering play of events: "Travis Walton himself is a very impressive witness. He discusses his experience with subdued descriptions—he tries to be complete and factual when responding to questions. . . . [He] is puzzled by some of his experience, but he doesn't attempt to speculate and explain it.

"Dr. Sprinkle's impression of Travis is that of a young man who, although not highly educated, is a very astute observer, and willing to aid serious UFO research in any way possible. . . . He is by nature shy, and not the sort to seek attention. Although he has been described repeatedly in the press as a 'UFO buff' or student of UFOs, this has not been borne out by our investigation. Our findings are that he has a healthy curiosity about many things, including UFOs, but had never bought a book on the subject, or joined a UFO organization—in fact, he did not know that such organizations existed."

Nor did he, apparently, recognize the name of Dr. J. Allen Hynek—one of the most eminent men in the field of UFology, and director of Northwestern University's Astronomy Department. Hynek was the man Walton refused to see at Bill Spaulding's behest. The refusal only added fuel to the fires of the hoax-criers.

Walton finally wrote to Hynek, expressing some dismay at his previous ignorance, and generally discussing his own thoughts and feelings on the case to date.

Hynek replied:

Thank you for your recent letter. I feel that I know you a little better now, since I saw you on TV a short time ago, and since I was on the same NBC news show with you, perhaps you also feel as if we have been introduced.

While I agree with you completely that needless duplication in science is to be avoided, it has been my practice in the some twenty-five years that I have been associated with the UFO problem to try, whenever possible, to get to know the witnesses to UFO sightings personally. No amount of written material is quite the same as the feeling of authenticity and confirmation of a case one gets when one can bring his own years of experience into direct contact with the witnesses. This is particularly important in this case, since I have had so many comments [one from Dr. Wood, at Arizona State University] to the effect that the entire Snowflake incident was a hoax. I do not personally believe this, but it makes it all the more important not to accept anyone else's word; I prefer to base my conclusions on personal conversation with the principals involved.

Dr. Hynek suggested that he and Travis get together to discuss the case in an informal and friendly manner.

Travis replied:

I am glad you are not one of the many armchair researchers I've heard from since my experience. These "scientists" conduct their entire investigations from behind their desks, basing their conclusions on incomplete hearsay and erroneous newspaper reports. None of these men has had a personal interview with me or my fellow crew members.

I would be happy to meet with you when you come to Arizona on the nineteenth. I would like to meet with you at my home in Snowflake, if possible, as I would be financially inconvenienced by a drive to Phoenix. I'll try to have with me as many of the workers who witnessed the encounter as can make it. Perhaps you would also be interested in meeting with representatives of APRO when you are in Phoenix.

In the meantime, I may be able to find a way to get to Phoenix on the nineteenth. Please let me hear from you in advance to confirm our meeting.

Thus, Travis and Dr. Hynek finally met. After their private interview, and after studying the evidence available to him, Dr. Hynek publicly announced: "He is not hoaxing. He is being falsely accused of hoax."

Thereby, Hynek rebuked one of his own field investigators, Bill Spaulding, who had publicly labeled the case a complete hoax. According to Travis, Hynek told him: "I guess I sent the wrong man in on this one."

APRO agreed with the conclusion. But APRO was not disposed to so easily let Spaulding off the hook. Instead, it wanted some answers from Spaulding about large issues raised by him and Steward in the Travis Walton case.

First, there was the litany of condemnatory statements attributed to them in press reports. Second, there was Spaulding's claim that he had discovered high degrees of residual magnetism at the alleged abduction site. Third, and perhaps most intriguing, there was a matter of a pile of metal fragments allegedly found by Spaulding at the site. Exactly what were these fragments? And what did they have to do with the UFO?

According to the Waltons, Spaulding had produced them after he had been removed from the case in the aftermath of the abortive Steward "medical" arrangements. The Waltons believed that the metal fragments were, at best, a ploy by which Spaulding sought to regain their confidence, their acceptance, their goodwill—he wanted back on the case, so he produced the metal fragments.

Mary Walton Kellet said that there were half a dozen pieces black and shiny, each about as big as a fingernail. "Frankly," she said, "we were skeptical of them. Nobody saw him gather them, and he didn't say anything about them until after Duane had decided not to have anything further to do with him. To me, they just looked like pieces of somebody's busted-up motor. They didn't look like anything at all. But he was all excited about them. He said he picked them up out there, right where Travis had been taken. He was supposed to have them checked at a laboratory in California."

Finally, after a series of less than cordial letters from the Lorenzens, Spaulding responded.

The main objective of his letter was to clarify three important matters concerning the Walton case. Number 1 was the residual magnetism which was discovered by two field investigators using Anis TM Gauss meters. Spaulding had verified the presence of the magnetism himself. He sent the Lorenzens a grid map of the search location and added that the magnetic anomaly had, strangely, dissipated to a normal reading a week after the initial reading. The second matter that Spaulding wanted to clarify had to do with the metal fragments that were found near the purported landing site. An analysis showed the fragments to be silicone and thus highly heat resistant. Spaulding conjectured that it appeared to be the type of metal which is utilized in electronic insulation application and suggested that someone might have "dropped" the material at the site. Lastly, Spaulding stated that the consultant staff at GSW alluded to "the [many] misquotes in print media" and believed that there was an actual sighting. He felt that the polygraph testing of the witnesses and the secondary evidence supported this opinion. However, they did not believe that there had been an abduction. Spaulding gave the Lorenzens no particular justification for this opinion except that it was based on a multitude of facts and reasons that did not include Dr. Steward's judgment.

So much for Steward.

As for Spaulding, Mary Walton Kellet delivered her final judgment: "We just happened to run into him out at the search. He seemed to be quite nice when we talked to him. He was certainly hot to trot and everything. I don't know about his qualifications. I'm not going to say he's not qualified to investigate these things. I don't know how you get to be qualified for something like this. But I will say that I think he has a lot to learn. . . ."

So the most visible critics of the abduction tale, the anti-Walton forces, were in sad disarray. They desperately needed a new champion.

And far away, in Washington, one was horsing up, heavily armed with barbed lances. He fairly snorted at the bit, preparing to gallop into the fray. His name was Philip Klass, a man who had acquired, what he considered, large substance as an expert in the field of UFOs. He wrote books that claimed to prove that UFOs did not exist. And he had made offers of a ten-thousand-dollar reward to anyone who could also prove their non-existence.

Klass entered the lists against the Travis Walton story.

So as the winter snows of the high country faded off toward spring thaw, the fallout over Snowflake from the UFO skies was far from over.

12.

MARY WALTON KELLET HAD VISIONS. "PSYCHIC PHENOM-
ena" was Dr. Harder's allusion to them. Precognition was
the psychiatric label. And there also was less kindly jargon
bandied about.

Mary herself thought that the less said about the subject, the better. People would only twist it into the distorted view that they already had of herself and her
family. Outsiders would. Many Mormons, however, would
tend to understand. A vision, after all, had been responsible for the founding of the Mormon religion.

In 1827, a New York farmer named Joseph Smith
claimed that an angel had appeared to him and led him
to a set of golden tablets buried in the earth. The tablets
were inscribed with strange writing. Smith's vision said
that the Prophet Mormon had inscribed the tablets with
the record of an ancient people. Smith was directed to
translate their history. He did so, and in 1830 it was published as the *Book of Mormon*.

The *Book* claimed that the original American Indians
were descended from the Lost Tribes of Israel, and that
all peoples were derived from one sacred race of creators.

Smith established the Mormon Church in Fayette, New
York. As his small flock grew, it moved westward, to
Ohio, then to Missouri. Driven by persecution from Mis-
souri, it came to Illinois, founding the city of Nauvoo.
Other settlers feared both Mormon success and Mormon
ways.

Smith and his brother were murdered in 1844. The
Mormons were driven farther west, into Mexican territory.

In 1847, they founded a haven for all Mormons on the Great Salt Lake. They were the first whites to irrigate the desert lands, using methods rooted in the ancient Indian cultures of the Aztec, the Inca, the Maya, and the Toltec. These were cultures steeped in astronomical skills and beliefs. The Inca believed that they had descended from Inti, the sun. Other tribes believed that the original spirits had come from the sky, the moon, and the morning and evening stars—from whence came the first men and women.

From their surviving artifacts, sculptures, and dwellings, modern theorists have devised a speculative thesis—that all the ancient cultures emanated from the first spacemen.

Thereby, great inexplicable markings on the earth become "landing sites" laid out by these first astronauts. The mile-high solar stone at Macchu Picchu becomes an astronomical control tower. Fiery objects chiseled into stone are discerned as replicas of the first space capsules. Helmeted figures, also carved into stone, are identified as the space travellers who emerged from those capsules.

And, to these theorists, it is not inconceivable that that is where the golden tablets of Mormon first came from— from the ancient astronauts who journeyed to the earth in their "chariots of the gods."

However, as noted by T. S. Eliot, "Between the idea and the reality . . . falls the shadow." Only the tangible fact of irrigation methods remains to link such a gulf of time and distance and culture. The method mastered by the early Mormons on the western Indian lands was the same as that practiced by the tribes thousands of miles south, and centuries before the Spanish explorers first arrived. How that specific skill transversed continents and cultures is not known.

Nevertheless, it certainly was not a mystery that intruded upon the life of Mary Walton Kellet. Though she was Indian, and Mormon, her visions did not strike her as being connected to any special supernatural or primogenitor force. There were simply times when she knew that something had gone wrong with one of her kin, someone was in trouble, endangered. Sometimes she knew exactly who was imperiled; sometimes she only knew the exact peril.

Thus, at six-fifteen on the night when Travis disappeared, she began pacing up and down at the Bear Creek ranch, smoking faster, pacing faster. Something was wrong with Travis, she knew, but she didn't know what. She just knew that he was in danger.

At six-fifteen that night, Travis was struck by a blue-green ray of light fired out of the bottom of a flying saucer, or so it seemed to Mike Rogers' crew.

When Travis was still a baby, he slipped soundlessly into a tub of water. Mary was in another part of the house, but she immediately sensed that something was wrong. She ran to the tub and pulled Travis out. His body was turning black. She pumped him out and he resumed breathing.

When Duane was still a child, he was playing on a backyard swing one day. Someone knocked on the front door and Mary went to answer. It was her boyfriend. She opened the door, and suddenly, without any tangible warning, she spun around and raced to the back of the house. Duane was coming through the back door, with the top part of his head gashed open, the scalp hanging loose. He had fallen out of a tree. Mary clapped the scalp back into place with her hand and then rushed Duane to the hospital, thus saving him from bleeding to death.

Sometimes her sense of inner forewarning was translated into precise pictures, as happened when one son was in Vietnam. She suddenly visualized him standing in a pool of blood. She saw his face and she saw the pool of blood. Beyond that, though, she didn't know what had happened. Two weeks later, she received a letter from him:

> Everything's all right now, Mom. . . . They tried to shoot my damned feet off.

She wrote back that she had been worried sick, and why didn't he let her know as soon as he found out he was okay?

Closer to home, she was asleep at the ranch one day, and she dreamed of a car-truck accident. She awoke with a start, then immediately drove to Snowflake, checking with each of her family to make sure they were all right. The Neffs had gone to a nearby town to pick up a load of cinder blocks. On their way back, the brakes on their car-truck failed, and it rolled over with all the kids inside. None was hurt.

Late one afternoon she was alone in the Snowflake house when she began to feel nervous, upset, for no apparent reason. She visualized her father, and then she knew that he was dead. About six o'clock, Duane came home. She looked at his drawn face and said, "I know. My father's dead, isn't he? He died about an hour ago."

Duane nodded. "Has somebody been here to tell you?" he asked.

"No. I just knew it."

On another occasion, Travis was working with a fire-fighting crew. Mary abruptly sensed that he was in danger. Something had happened, or was about to happen, to him. She began her frantic pacing and smoking, waiting to find out how bad it was. He called her that night and said that just before he had gone out on a job, he had a strong feeling that he was not coming back. He had been certain that he was going to die in the woods that day.

"Yes, I picked that up," she told him. "But I only got half the message, the wrong half. I didn't get the part when you did come back all right."

So these were Mary's visions. Where they came from, she didn't know, and wouldn't guess. She was even hesitant to discuss them. But the fact of them was part of the "psychic phenomena" that Dr. Harder had noted in the Walton family background. Like previous UFO interest, such previous psychic involvement also served to forewarn investigators of tainted tales.

Mary took a more practical view. "These were things that happened; I don't know how, and I don't know why. I do know that some of them taught me to keep a hold on myself during an emergency. I don't get hysterical. I react to trouble with something that will solve the problem. I don't know how I knew that Travis was under the water in that tub, or that Duane had split his head open falling out of that tree. But I do know that if I'd just gone hysterical, they might have both died right there. I raised six of my own children, and five that weren't my own, and you don't do that by going to pieces when one of them gets hurt. You hang on to everything until everything's under control.

"So when Travis was gone, the deputies just couldn't understand why I didn't go into hysterics. None of them could understand why I didn't fall apart. I didn't because it's not my way, and because that wouldn't help anything. They couldn't understand that.

"Some of them started saying, well, she's in on it, she's hiding him, it's nothing but a big hoax. Some called me a UFO buff. I had never seen a UFO—I've only seen these lights dashing across the sky at night. I had never seen a UFO, as far as I knew, and I had never read an article about them.

"Well, when they kept attributing all these kind of stories to me, accusing me, the children said: 'Mother would you be interested in taking a polygraph test?' I said yes, because I have nothing to hide. And I was not hiding my son. I knew nothing other than what I'd been told. And I believed just like Mike told me. I believed every word of it. I had no reason to question it. I guess that's why they called me a UFO buff—because I believed the story, I believed the boys' story, and I believed Travis when he came back.

"So I did take a polygraph test, on these facts and stories, and I passed one hundred percent. They asked me did I hide him, did I see him during the five days he was gone, did I know where he was during that time, did I harbor him? They asked me if I was a UFO buff, or if I had read any books about UFOs. I had never, and even to this day I have not.

"They asked me anything I had been accused of, that was slanderous. They asked me about all the charges, so I could deny them or acknowledge them. I did not fail on any one of them.

"We had seen lights out at the ranch. Even yet we see them. Even from town you can see them. They are like a light that comes straight down, and then it goes *pffft!*—straight out at a complete right angle. They can come in that way, or go up—just in a flash, just a streak. I don't think that anything we have is that sophisticated."

Had she told Sank Flake that she had watched a whole fleet of them swooping in and out at the ranch one night?

"No whole fleet, no—isolated ones. We have seen them

from that point, and even from the house in Snowflake. One, but not no fleets, never. In fact, I don't even look at the sky anymore. Oh, I look up there and say, gee, aren't those stars beautiful. And then I get back into my house real quick.

"So we had seen these lights ourselves. But we didn't say what they were. We didn't know what they were. People have told me that they have seen these things, still see them. Probably the biggest percentage of them believe that there is something there, more than you would find in most communities, because they have seen these lights. But there is no explanation for them. The biggest percentage of your people here are very devout, very religious people. And I think, like me, they wonder: Why these things? What about them? They can't just say they're not there when they've seen something.

"I honestly don't know what they are. I have never said that I do know. Then all these stories started coming out about me. The polygraph report said I was telling the truth, completely. The only thing was . . . I had feelings of animosity against Marlin Gillespie, the sheriff. And why?

"Frankly, because he sat out there [during the search] and told me of two or three incidents where he had seen flying objects come quite close to him. . . . And then he made the statement that I was a UFO buff! And that rubbed my fur the wrong way. And that was the only animosity that I showed on the test. It was not that I was lying. It was that I had a . . . uh . . . personal argument with the sheriff.

"His stories would have ruined him. His office is political. He's got an elected job, and he doesn't want to lose it by admitting that he knows there are UFOs.

"He told us of one incident—he was picking up a car. I assumed it was a stolen car or something. He and another driver were taking it back to Holbrook. And somewhere between Snowflake and Holbrook, one of these things came so low that the driver of the other car that was ahead of him just ran right off the road, because it excited him or whatever. And then they got the car back on the road and drove it to town. And he got somebody to go back with him, and it, this object, was still hanging somewhere at the side of the highway—a bright, lighted object. It was just sitting there.

"Then during two other incidents, when he was hunting, he and his hunting buddies had seen these things. They had come fairly low over the car, and then they just took off, *pffft!* Lighted objects. So when he called me a UFO buff, that just rubbed me the wrong way, because I had never come that close to anything that could be called a UFO. But then everybody in the press picks up on that, UFO buffs, like we're all nuts, hallucinating, or hoaxing, or something like that.

"We have seen these lights for years, and almost everyone around here has seen them. But that doesn't make us UFO buffs. It certainly doesn't give us a reason for creating a hoax. We had no reason for that. And we sure don't have the money it would take to manufacture what all these six witnesses say they saw.

"I have no reason whatsoever to doubt all the witnesses' stories, or no reason whatsoever to doubt Travis. I was no party to any kind of hoax. No. I wouldn't stand for it in a minute. And I don't think my children would be capable of doing a thing like that to begin with. And it would cost too darned much money. There's just not that kind of money around."

Mary, as it happened, had known Gillespie prior to Travis' disappearance.

"He's a very nice man, and I had met him through friends a few years back, when he was a deputy. He's always seemed a very nice gentleman. Even the polygraph asked, one of the questions was: 'Was this a personal thing, because you were at one time his girl friend?' I said: 'Heck, no!' [She shook with great, hearty laughter.] The thing that irritated me was that he called me a UFO buff, and I am not. I was not, and I am not.

"This was an incident in our lives that I hope would never happen again. I wouldn't want anybody to go through it. It was quite an ordeal, wondering what had happened to Travis. I'm a mother who raised six children by herself. And anything that concerns my six children, and upsets them, or hurts them, I am concerned with.

"I have a very honest bunch of young people. My family are LDS [Latter Day Saints]—not too active in the church. But they knew there were two things they would get skinned alive for—and those were lying or stealing. I really did bear down on them for those. They grew up big enough to defend their stories and tell the truth. Travis, I think, is a fairly good physical specimen. Duane is bigger than he is. I just didn't tolerate lying. And they're big enough to stand up for themselves, if they're accused, or something.

"My children have all been very close to each other. Oh, they're like all children. They'll fight among themselves, argue. I think this is par for the course for brothers and sisters. But they're behind each other one hundred percent. Oh, they'll criticize each other, but they don't want anybody else to do it.

"So when Travis came back, of course he was still upset. It was quite an ordeal for him, too. Anybody can understand that. Anybody is going to be scared after a thing like that, and suspicious of being hurt more. Which is why Duane took over. We had already had so much harassment—from the news media, and some policemen, just everything.

"I stayed out of it. I was hurt. I had raised my six children by myself, and it was not an easy struggle, working practically eighteen hours a day. And since my children have grown up, they are quite protective of me. And they figured that all this did was hurt me, and I didn't need anymore.

"I have to accept it that he [Travis] was abducted for five days, abducted by an unidentified flying object, whatever it might be. I did not see him, and I did not know of his whereabouts during those five days. And it was quite an ordeal. Any mother who even got a message that her son was reported missing, in action overseas, that would be quite a trauma. And my children thought I had suffered enough.

"So Duane took over. He protected Travis and . . . you can't even get Duane to talk about UFOs anymore, period. He belligerently hit the press right and left, verbally. He didn't hit 'em physically; this would be against the law. He is six-feet-three, and he's a professional boxer. He works out in his own gym. He doesn't drink and he doesn't smoke. He is a boxer and a rodeo bull-rider. So he's a good healthy specimen. Travis doesn't smoke or drink coffee, either one. But Duane is really the biggest one, and quite imposing when he gets his anger up. He let all of them know exactly what was on his mind when the worst of this was going on.

"All the hurt, the mean things that've been said about this family . . . you'd have to be out of your mind to dream up something like this and get this involved if it didn't really happen. We like our privacy. We're just an ordinary American family. But this really was . . . I don't even know how to describe how some people were acting toward us. When the press from London got here, I just went out the back door of my own house and kept going.

"And we found out later that telephones of people we knew were being tapped. Of course, no one will ever admit to that. This strictly was illegal. Travis did make the call to my daughter that night he came back, and it was not monitored. If it had been, the police and everybody would have been here. And they did not know about it until later that day. But we understood later that there was some tapping of telephones.

"It was just a very hard time, with what people were saying, and how they were acting, even while Travis was still gone. But the people here have been very kind, even the ones who couldn't believe such a thing. The neighbors here—they would come over and ask if they could do anything for the family. And they said they would be praying for Travis and the family. The ones right here were very kind, trying to be helpful. And we are not that well known here. We have not been here that long, not one of the settler families, like so many are.

"This one woman who did not believe in UFOs, she saw an ad in a magazine, something like: HAVE YOU SEEN UFOS? CALL THIS NUMBER. So she called the number—it was up in the state of Washington—and she explained what was going on. And then it went down to Flagstaff, and then to Tucson . . . and that was how APRO got in touch with us. Because this woman was trying to help, and she figured, well, I'll call this number and maybe they'll know something to help out here. And she said she really couldn't believe in UFOs, but that was not the point."

Other "neighbors" had not been so kind, however. Sank Flake, for one, had amply expressed his blunt view of the entire affair. He also said that on the morning before the return, he had gone to the house with a message, and Mary wouldn't let him in—like she was hiding something inside. Sank thought that maybe Travis was already in there.

Mary said she didn't recall the incident.

"But I had been refusing to invite them in for two or three days, after Duane found me crying, with one of the deputies just sitting there talking, talking, talking. Duane told me to meet them at the door and not let them inside anymore, for my own protection, so I could leave when I wanted to. They just couldn't seem to understand how this thing was tearing us up. They would just keep sitting there, hashing and rehashing it, over and over again. Katie Rogers practically had to throw them out of her house, it got so bad."

Katie said there was no practically about it. "I did throw them out."

And then there were the crank calls, progressively crueler and more malicious.

"Duane was threatened to be killed," Mary said. "Not me. I didn't put my phone back on until much later, and then it was under a different name. Allison got a lot of bad calls. For months there, Duane got calls in the middle of the night—'We're going to kill you,' and so forth, all kinds of threats. He told the police, so they came out there to his house. But they said there was not much that they could do.

"So Duane says to them: 'I want to tell you—I sleep with a gun close enough to me so that if anybody breaks into my house, he is a *dead* duck!'"

Travis, she figured, had survived the whole ordeal fairly well.

"He's tried to cooperate. He doesn't have anything to hide. So he goes on the radio, or television, when he's asked—maybe more than he should have, more times than I can count. But he's handled it pretty well. There are many things about the experience that he can't explain, and he doesn't try. Some of it still bothers him, like the missing time. But he's adjusted to it all fairly well."

When she was first told that her son was gone, according to one report she replied: "Why my child?" With the passage of healing time, she viewed the question with considerable humor.

"That's what he gets for being so darned nosy. He has . . . all of his life . . . he has always had to know why. When he was little, if he heard something that puzzled him, he'd say: 'Well, Momma, why?' He's always been curious as to how things work, and why. That's the only thing I could think of—why him? He just wanted to see what that thing looked like. That would be my opinion now. Just interested—what did it look like? He wanted to see underneath that thing, to see what it really did look like. He was the only one, obviously, interested or curious enough to go over and look. He wasn't panicked at that point. And I don't think the other fellows really were until something happened to Travis.

"He was just the only one who was dumb enough to run over there by it. If the whole mess of them had gotten out of that truck and run over there, they'd have probably taken the whole bunch of them. . . ."

And that was a sentiment with which Travis himself wholeheartedly agreed: "I was just dumb enough to get that close. I don't feel singled out. There was nothing special about me. It was just a matter of chance, my being there. And I was dumb enough to go over there near it."

13.

IF THERE WAS NOTHING VERY SPECIAL ABOUT TRAVIS
Walton, he was not exactly ordinary, either. Nor was his
mother, his brother, or "the whole bunch of them" who
had witnessed the beginnings of the alleged UFO abduction.

It seemed to gall some investigators that these people
were not typical. They could not be jammed into a safe
and reassuring stereotype. They would not be simple,
quiet, humble, tongueless, feckless, ignorant, dim-witted
backwoods mountain people, trembling and impaled by
their own rustic astonishment at what had happened. Had
they been such wooden caricatures, they would have
thereby become believable.

Instead, Travis and his mother and his brother and
most of the Mike Rogers' forestry crew were highly in-
dividualistic human beings who could think and talk and
act with intelligence and imagination. They had personality, even some flamboyance. Therefore, they were suspect,
condemned by their own human traits. The detractors
simply could not disprove the Walton story by more credible methods; they could not assemble the known facts
into an irrefutable chain of cause-and-effect evidence.

The Waltons and the witnesses were, on one hand, the
strength of the story; and on the other, they were the
weakness. Surely, as the pressure built over a year, one
of them would crack, confess, blow the lid off the whole
deal, spill the beans, let the cat out of the bag. Somebody
would get caught in an unguarded moment, bragging.
Somebody would surely just plain slip up.

But who?

The weakest links seemed to be Dwayne Smith, Allen Dalis, Steve Pierce, and John Goulette. They were considered the "minor" characters in the tale, without strong ties to the major figures, with little to gain from perpetuating a fraud, possibly with something to gain from exposing such a fraud. A bit of money might be made from revealing the "hoax." And a bit of fame might be earned, as well.

Smith was from Phoenix. He had been working with the crew for only three days when the UFO encounter occurred. All he knew is what he saw, he claimed—just what all the others saw. Dr. Harder hypnotized him, seeking verification. But the preliminary approach was not followed up with full regression. Smith remained adamant with his story.

"We saw a spaceship out there. And I do not have any doubt about it. Travis jumped out of the truck, ran over toward it, and it got him. He just vanished. He went on it. He went on that spaceship. There's no doubt of that in my mind."

Smith returned to Phoenix, unshaken in his belief, unwavering in his attestation.

Allen Dalis was also hypnotized. Dr. Harold Cahn regressed him to the time of the UFO confrontation. Dalis vividly described cringing on the back floor of the truck, terrified as he knelt on the floorboards and peeked out the window at the awesome sight of the glowing UFO.

Dalis also departed Snowflake for Phoenix. Unlike Smith he did not disappear in anonymity. Instead, he got caught in the act of robbing a Phoenix councilman's home. Convicted of armed robbery, he was imprisoned in the Arizona State Penitentiary. Authorities said that Dalis copped out, confessed to everything that he had ever done in his life. But he stuck to his UFO story absolutely.

His father said that Allen just seemed to have gone blooey after that *thing* happened in the woods. Others were not so sure that the UFO could be blamed for Allen's problems. For one, Mike Rogers thought that Allen had been headed for disaster long before the rattling experience at Turkey Springs. Even Sank Flake agreed with that estimation.

Meanwhile, Steve Pierce was also headed for trouble, but of a different kind. He was the kid of the crew, just seventeen, and not noted for strength of will or mind. After the shattering event in the woods, Pierce married his teen-age sweetheart. They were not destined to live happily ever after.

Sheriff Gillespie's deputy in Taylor was Jim Click, the former town marshal. A curious relationship began to develop between Pierce and Deputy Click. Though separated by much more than just a generation gap, they became friends and spent more and more time together. They discussed Steve's difficult personal life. And they discussed the Travis Walton case.

Finally, a rumor leaked: Steve has recanted.

According to Sank Flake, "Click has a signed denial from Steve Pierce that says it [the UFO incident] never happened. Click wants to be the one to break the case, because he wants to run for sheriff. I don't know if he's solved it or not. He says he has."

According to Mike Rogers, "Steve told me and Travis that he had been offered ten thousand dollars just to sign a denial. He said he was thinking about taking it. We asked him, 'Even though you know it happened, would you deny it, just for the money?' He said maybe he would; he was thinking about it. So I told him, 'Then you'll spend the money alone, and you'll be bruised.'"

The fact was, Steve was already bruised inside himself. Out of work, penniless, his not overly strong personality was cracking. The proffered money might have turned his whole life around. But he didn't take it, and he signed no denial. Instead, he fled the high plateau in misery and panic, a man-child dispossessed by his own personal devils.

Though the sheriff's office refused comment on the denial-for-money story, Deputy Click candidly admitted that an offer had been made. He refused to say who had made it.

"I just passed the word along from a friend," Click said. "I told Steve that if you can prove beyond a shadow of a doubt that it was a hoax, then you can make some money. You have to prove it."

Which was not what Steve had allegedly told Mike and Travis; the money was offered for a denial, not proof. No conditions had been attached; he did not have to prove anything.

As for who had offered such a large sum of money, it was extremely doubtful that the mysterious benefactor was a member of Snowflake's less-than-affluent society. Was it Philip Klass, and his standard offer of ten thousand dollars to anyone who could disprove the existence of UFOs?

Deputy Click remained steadfast in his refusal to reveal the source of the offer. But he did describe the evolution of his relationship with Steve Pierce.

"This is a boy who has no confidence in himself. He is a scared kid, and a slow learner. He had to take his driver's test two or three times before he passed it. I didn't know him much before this happened—this UFO in the woods. But afterward we started getting together. Over a peroid of months, we became good friends. I guess I became a kind of second father to him, because he needed someone. He's not a strong boy.

"I talked to him intensively about it—this UFO story—over a long period of time. He didn't know what to make of it. Then he said he was interested in revealing some things to me. Things were going pretty badly and he was having a difficult time. He came over to the house and wanted to borrow some money. I said, no, I couldn't do that, but that I'd fix him a good breakfast, and we'd talk, see what we could work out.

"I don't know what happened. He just left. He couldn't have had more than a couple of bucks in his pocket, if he had anything. Anyway, he was gone, and I couldn't find him anywhere. He just wasn't around anymore. I guess he went on down to Phoenix looking for his wife. His wife had gone down there when she left him.

"Over the months of my talking with him, he seemed certain that he did see something out in those woods. He definitely felt that he saw something. But after a while, he began to have doubts about what he saw. He felt it might have been a fabrication. There were some time elements there.

"Travis was gone most of the day, gone from the job. And another man, Mike Rogers, was gone for about two hours. And then they came back together. Steve was just at a loss to explain what happened. He is not too educated. He has a hard time expressing himself. He has indicated doubts, but to what degree, I don't know.

"We'd like to prove [the story] factual, or not factual. Possibly it could be a hoax. Maybe it's feasible, but it's highly improbable. But, as far as Steve goes, he didn't deny the story. He expressed some doubts, and we just never got to the bottom of them. He got nothing out of it, and he gets nothing without proof."

There was no proof. Deputy Click did not "crack the case." Steve Pierce got no money from the secret bankroller. Instead, Pierce joined the army and left the state.

During the long months of his "discussions" with Jim Click, Pierce had expressed his "doubts" in connection with a previously unnoted accusation—Travis, he said, was gone from the job most of the day, and Mike was gone for about two hours. When they returned, they returned together.

The implication, though not stated, was clear: Travis and Mike could have been off in the woods "fabricating" the UFO.

Mike Rogers bluntly called Pierce "a liar. I was not gone from the job that day, or any other day, not for two hours or any other amount of time. Travis had been sick the day before, and he spent some time that morning lying in the truck. But he spent the rest of the day working with the crew."

John Goulette confirmed Mike's version. And he added, "The truck is never very far away, usually not even out of sight. They move it up, keep it close to the crew. We keep all our lunches and stuff in it. That day I think we took two breaks: one halfway through the morning, and one halfway through the afternoon.

"Nobody left the work site. We were cutting pretty well all along a line. The pilers come up right behind us. They pile [the debris] right behind us. You know, if you're out working, working pretty hard, and you see somebody else goofing off, you kind of notice if they're not there. You think they're out messing around. Nobody's going to put up with that—if you're sweating away and somebody else is goofing off.

"Nobody was gone that day. It's not true that Travis and Mike took off, or something, and then came back a couple of hours later together."

Goulette was one of the witnesses who claimed to have seen the saucer fire a blue-green ray of light into Travis.

"It was like static electricity, but it wasn't jagged; it was like a solid beam. It hit Travis, and I looked at Mike, probably screaming to get the hell out of here. When I looked back, Travis was falling to the ground. I thought he was dead, or something."

Accusations had been made that Travis had primed the work crew with UFO stories, that the crew talked about it all the time.

"It came up some," Goulette admitted. "We talked about it some, maybe once or twice. Travis had said that if he ever saw one out there, he'd try to communicate with it. I don't know . . . coming home from the woods, it's pretty dark, driving down lonely roads. It's kind of nice to play with each other's imaginations, like kids tell ghost stories. It just came up because it's something kind of scary.

"On this job, I worked for about a month and a half. I was living down in the valley [Phoenix] for a while. I had worked for Mike before. But I had only been on this job for about a month and a half. And over that time, UFOs came up maybe three times, at the most.

"Mostly it was just Mike and Travis arguing about what would make them fly. Mike and Travis always argued a lot. They were good friends, but they liked to argue with each other. They're both pretty intelligent and well spoken. One would have a theory, and then the other one would argue another theory. Then we'd all talk about something else. Nobody was obsessed with UFOs. It was just something that came up. We saw what we saw, and it wasn't any story that Travis told us. It was real."

Could he have been duped by a hoax?

"No, I don't think so."

Did he believe that he actually saw a UFO?

"Yeah, I know I did."

Did he believe that Travis was taken aboard the UFO?

"Yeah, I'm pretty positive. I can't say I'm one-hundred-percent positive, because I didn't see him go aboard. I just can't think of any other way he could have stayed out in those woods for five days. It's too cold. There's nothing to eat. Travis might know a lot, but he isn't no Euell Gibbons, to stay out there eating nuts and berries for five days.

"The reason I don't think it was a hoax was because

163

it looked so perfect. I've never seen such a perfect shape. It seemed like there was nothing, just nothing wrong with it—the way it sat in the air, and then it started the low, rumbling noise, and started rocking back and forth. . . . You could see there was nothing holding it up.

"It was about fifteen or twenty feet off the ground. And those trees out there, they're pine trees. All the limbs down the bottom die out. They log through there, and they've taken most of the bigger timber out. Mostly it's smaller trees, maybe about twenty feet tall, but they wouldn't hold up any weight at all. They'd bend right over.

"This thing was hovering in the clearing, away from the trees. Maybe there was one tree large enough, but I think it was a ways to the side, not close. Somebody said there could have been a rope hanging up there, but I don't see how they'd get it up there. There's nothing to climb on. And I don't know of any power out there, so where did the lights and sound come from? What made the thing rock back and forth like that? People just don't realize what this thing looked like if they think it was just something strung up in the trees."

But some people had suggested that maybe the UFO looked like more than it actually was because the crew was high.

"No," Goulette replied. "It had nothing to do with drugs. You can't mess around with drugs and work with chainsaws. You'd cut yourself pretty bad. There's just not that much of it [drugs] up here anyway. I don't mess around with anything like cocaine, acid, or anything like that. I will smoke pot every once in a while, but never when working. You just can't do it and work, too. And Travis and Mike and Kenny Peterson wouldn't never do it, anyway. They're into health stuff. No drugs—nobody was even drinking beer. No intoxicants or drugs were involved at all."

The police investigation confirmed that Travis, Mike, and Ken Peterson appeared to be strict abstainers—no drugs, no alcohol. They did not smoke. They abstained even from coffee and Coke because of their caffeine content. Travis and Mike were known adherents of the rigid physical discipline surrounding the study and practice of karate.

Of the seven-man work crew, only Allen Dalis appeared to have a background of repeated drug usage.

Goulette had been one of three men absolutely refusing to return to the "abduction" site on the night that Travis disappeared. With Pierce and Smith, he appeared to have been most visibly shaken by the experience, emotionally decimated, frightened, confused, and possibly permanently damaged by psychological trauma. However, he became one of the more successful survivors of the episode, devoid of any lingering fears, apparently not even overly impressed by it all as time put a secure distance between himself and the event.

"I'm glad I saw it and everything," he said. "And I know I saw it. I know it happened. But it's not really that important to me anymore. It's something good to bring up as a conversation, something to talk about. You know, almost everybody knows about a UFO case—you tell them your experience, and they tell you theirs. That's about all I ever use it for.

"I had never had much interest in it before. I don't think I had heard of other incidents, though one time Travis and I were going over to Shumway—that's a small town on the other side of Taylor, off a side road. There seemed to be a light or something just above the car. But it was just for a little bit. We really thought nothing of it. We didn't think too much about it at all. That's the only incident I knew of before this other one happened. Then after, I heard of a few.

"I knew they existed, or believed they existed. But they just didn't concern me. I had nothing to do with them until that time. I knew they were there, but I really didn't think much about them. If they had been seen a lot, and had been doing terrible things to people, I imagine I'd be pretty concerned. But I've never heard of anyone being really hurt, taken away forever, or something like that."

Thus, the weak links turned out to be quite strong, after all. The only "break" had been Steve Pierce. And the circumstances surrounding his reputed abnegation had compromised him completely, not only for then, but for good.

In fact, for those few people who knew about it, the offer to pay Pierce for his denial was not exactly viewed as an honorable deed. There was a stench about it, and a sordidness.

Mindful of certain statutes, it was not without good legal reason that the sheriff's department declined comment on the offer—neither denying nor confirming it. It was a potential bombshell that could have blown both Gillespie and his deputy, Click, clean out of the Navajo County political waters. Along the Mogollon frontier, fair play and integrity still counted for something in the minds and hearts of decent citizens. And the Travis Walton case was not excepted from the frontier code.

14.

"THE ALLEGED UFO ABDUCTION OF TRAVIS WALTON ON November 5, 1975, in the Apache–Sitgreaves National Forest [Arizona] is a hoax, and the claims of six other young wood-cutters that they saw the alleged incident are not true."

Thus wrote Philip Klass in a seventeen-page copyrighted report of his six-month investigation of the case.

Not only was the Walton story a hoax, Klass charged, but the hoax was also covered up.

"Evidence that the incident was a hoax has long been known to APRO [Aerial Phenomena Research Organization], a large Tucson-based UFO group, and to the *National Enquirer* newspaper. This evidence has been withheld from APRO's membership and from the public."

The evidence was the McCarthy polygraph test, which Travis had flunked on November 15. According to McCarthy, Travis had "showed gross deception on the charts . . . he was deliberately attempting to distort his respiration pattern . . . [and] in concert with others, [he] is attempting to perpetrate a UFO hoax. . . . He has not been on any spacecraft."

Klass correctly reported that the failed lie-detector test was not included in accounts of the case published by both the *Enquirer* and APRO. But Klass did not report that the test had been ruled invalid by three psychiatrists, as well as other "experts" who considered Travis emotionally unfit for such testing at that time.

In an apparent direct attack on Travis' character and

167

credibility, Klass wrote: "During the private discussions between McCarthy and Travis Walton prior to the start of the formal examination, *Walton admitted that he and a friend had once been arrested for stealing payroll checks, forging signatures, and cashing the checks . . .* McCarthy also told me that during his pre-examination discussions with Travis Walton, Travis admitted that he had previously used pot, speed, and LSD." This led Klass directly to the implication that drugs had played a major role in the alleged UFO abduction.

Klass simply ignored verifiable evidence that Travis had grown up from his wayward juvenile days—he had had no recent scrapes with the law; he apparently had used no drugs since his teen-age experimental stage. Klass also failed to mention that the only reason McCarthy knew about the derogatory information was because Travis had volunteered it during the pre-test interview. It did not result from astute McCarthy sleuthing, as might be inferred from the Klass account.

Nor did Klass reveal that McCarthy violated his own oath of contract by disclosing the test and its results; worse, he broke the utter professional and contractual confidentiality of the pre-test interview.

McCarthy excused his own breach of ethics by stating: "I decided to break my silence because the *National Enquirer* is involved in complicity, which is detrimental to our profession."

APRO aptly responded: "A number of his peers feel that it is McCarthy's action that has damaged the image of the profession."

Klass noted: "It was not until nearly three months after Travis failed the McCarthy lie-detector test that he took another, whose results have been widely publicized because he seemingly passed with flying colors."

But, Klass claimed, that test was flawed. First, Travis had dictated the questions to be asked. Second, the results were not all that decisive.

According to Tom Ezell, boss of the testing firm: "Because of the dictation of questions to be asked, this test should be invalidated . . . [and] the reactions on the charts, to my way of interpretation, would not be readable. You would not be able to say if he [Travis Walton] is telling the truth or if he's lying."

The examiner, George Pfeifer, defended the test results. He had left Ezell's company by the time the new squabble broke out. But, Klass reported, "Pfeifer disclosed an even more 'curious' aspect of the Travis Walton test. . . . He said that when APRO's Lorenzen called to arrange the test, he only asked that Pfeifer test Duane Walton. There was no mention of Travis being present or being tested, Pfeifer told me. Only after Pfeifer had completed the test on Duane on the afternoon of February 7, and went out to inform APROs Lorenzen that Duane had passed, did Lorenzen then ask Pfeifer if he would test Travis Walton, also."

Further, *"There is ample evidence that Travis Walton told at least one falsehood during his February 7 test that Pfeifer failed to detect. . . . That question was:* 'Before November 5, 1975, were you a UFO buff?' Travis answered: 'No.' Pfeifer believes Travis believed he was telling the truth."

But during the McCarthy test, Travis was asked: "In the past, have you ever thought of riding in a UFO?" He answered yes, and the charts indicated that he was telling the truth.

Klass asked Dr. Kandell "whether Travis or Duane had indicated any previous interest in UFOs."

Kandell answered: "They admitted to that freely, that he [Travis] was a 'UFO freak,' so to speak. . . . He had made remarks that if he ever saw one, he'd like to go aboard."

To which Dr. Rosenbaum added: "Everybody in the family claimed that they had seen them [UFOs]. . . . He's been preoccupied with this almost all his life. . . . Then he made the comment to his mother just prior to this incident that if he was ever abducted by a UFO, she was not to worry because he would be all right."

Travis and his mother both denied that he had ever made such a comment. The comment, they said, was typical of the rumors being spread around the town and repeated by newsmen during Travis' disappearance.

This was true of another allegation—that Travis had watched the NBC television special, "The UFO Incident," which described the alleged 1961 abduction of Barney and Betty Hill. Klass repeated the charge that Travis had seen the show two weeks before his own alleged abduction, a charge originally made by Deputy Ken Coplan and denied by Travis.

Klass said, "If a UFO could abduct the Hills in New Hampshire, why couldn't a UFO abduct a wood-cutter in Arizona?" Klass said, "Travis Walton would be the logical 'victim.' His oft-expressed desire to ride in a UFO could explain his seemingly foolhardy act of running under the UFO. And his expertise in UFology, compared to other crew members, would make it easier for him to concoct a story about his experiences aboard a UFO."

The Klass report included the possible scenario that Travis had been hiding out in a cabin, driven there by Mike Rogers' crew, and provisioned nightly by Duane. There was not a shred of evidence to support such an implication. In fact, the known evidence contradicted the theory.

But Klass had been caught in the same dilemma of previous debunkers, repeatedly relying upon error, rumor, misconception, and falsehood as evidence.

Therefore, in the Klassian view, when Travis' mother quit the ranch cabin and returned to her home in Snowflake, "this would avoid visits by law enforcement officers." The fact was, law enforcement officers, especially Sank Flake, climbed all over the ranch cabin looking for signs of Travis. Not a trace of him was ever found there, or at any other cabin site checked out by authorities.

So, not surprisingly, corroboration for Klass' drug theory depended upon Dr. Lester Steward, the self-proclaimed drug expert, whose credentials consisted of an unaccredited mail-order diploma-mill doctorate.

According to Klass, Steward observed that Travis was behaving like a drug user undergoing withdrawal. "More important, Steward had observed the small puncture wound on the inside of Travis' right elbow. This prompted Steward to suspect that Travis might have injected LSD, perhaps in combination with an animal tranquilizer called PCP, Steward later told me."

Travis did have a small "two-mm red spot in the crease of his right elbow, which was suggestive of a needle puncture," as described in Dr. Kandell's medical evaluation. But Kandell had never suggested that the mark had been left by a narcotic injection, LSD or otherwise.

Rather, he thought the two- to six-day-old wound "was like the kind you get from a blood test, except that it was not overlying any significant blood vessel."

More importantly, Steward had not observed the wound at all, because on the morning of Travis' visit to Steward's office, Travis was wearing a long-sleeved shirt, and Steward made no physical examination of him then or at any other time.

Steward possessed exactly no evidence that Travis had been injected with LSD, PCP, or any other drug. And neither did Klass. The known evidence, though not absolutely conclusive, disputed unsubstantiated guesses that drugs had played a role in the alleged UFO experience.

Significantly, the Klass report included a promotional hype for the author's book, *UFOs Explained*.

And it expressed especial appreciation for Bill Spaulding's "considerable assistance in my investigation" for providing, among other materials, "copies of local newspaper clippings on the incident that were most helpful."

Both Spaulding and the local newspapers had hardly shown themselves to be unimpeachable sources for solid and verifiable evidence on which to make sound and reasoned judgments in the Travis Walton case.

Potshotting APRO and Jim and Coral Lorenzen for not knowing better, Klass wryly noted "that APRO is the oldest UFO organization in this country, and the Lorenzens are among the most experienced investigators of UFO cases."

APRO calmly replied: "Errors and misrepresentations are rampant in the Klass report. And in some instances they are pyramided to produce entirely false impressions." APRO cited as an example what it believed to be McCarthy's unprovable statements about Travis' alleged obsession with UFOs. These unprovable statements were further reinforced by a false quote from Dr. Howard Kandell to the same effect, and then used as a basis for discrediting Travis' normal psychological profile as established by the MMPI test.

Typical of many accusers, Klass did not go to "the scene of the crime" to investigate. He did not bother to interview the perpetrators: Travis, his mother, Mike Rogers, or the work crew. He did interview Duane Walton by long-distance telephone. His final report strongly implied that Duane had lied to him about several major issues in the case.

As for the six wood-cutters, who, according to Klass, also lied about the incident, their polygraph corroboration hinged upon "this single UFO-related question: 'Did you tell the truth about actually seeing a UFO last Wednesday when Travis Walton disappeared?' "

Five answered yes, truthfully; one was inconclusive in his full test.

Klass therefore deduced: "Celestial bodies are sometimes mistaken for UFOs. At the time of the Walton incident, the planet Jupiter was very bright in the early evening sky and would have been visible at six-fifteen P.M. This is *not* to suggest that Rogers and his crew honestly imagined that Travis had been zapped by Jupiter. But if they were all partners in a pre-arranged hoax, all might be able to answer yes to this one UFO-related question without displaying overt signs of telling a significant falsehood."

Klass' claim simply echoed the ignorance about polygraph testing as previously voiced by Dr. Bickel, whose entire hoax theory had been shot to shreds by the established facts.

The Gilson polygraph tests did not verify the complete UFO story. But they did establish that "these five men did see some object that they believe to be a UFO . . . [and] if an actual UFO did not exist and the UFO is a man-made hoax, five of these men had no prior knowledge of a hoax."

Nonetheless, Klass spurned that evidence and stated: "The testimony by Mike Rogers and the other five crew members has seemed to some to substantiate the UFO abduction story, because these six witnesses seemed to have no motive, other than possible friendship with Travis, to fabricate the story. *But investigation reveals that there was a motive, a strong financial motive, for all of them to collaborate in a hoax.*"

The motive was the behind-schedule Forest Service contract. The Klass theory maintained that the alleged UFO would allow Rogers to terminate the contract legally, and without monetary penalty.

The Forest Service equally maintained that such a

theory was nonsense. To this could be added Sheriff Gillespie's evidence that the work crew was hardly composed of friendly collaborators.

Klass also addressed himself to the "suspicious" behavior and conduct of the Waltons during Travis' absence. For good measure, he lumped in Mike Rogers' actions, which had not been adjudged suspect previously.

"One possible explanation for the reaction of Rogers and the members of his family," Klass said, "is that they knew the incident was a hoax and that Travis was safe in a terrestrial hideout, rather than aboard an extraterrestrial spacecraft that might be taking him to a distant world from which he might never return."

Klass' evidence proving a hoax was very weak. Sheriff Gillespie dismissed the entire Klass report with a single epitaph: "It is a collection of personal opinion and unsubstantiated theory."

Unfortunately, it was elsewhere reported that Philip Klass had torn the Walton abduction story to shreds. The story was a hoax and a fraud. Klass, after all, was a noted author, editor, and all-around anti-UFO expert. He had written a famous book pertinent to the issue: *UFOs Explained*.

News managers heel to reputation and credentials. Thus does the public acquire information on which to base opinion. And, so, who was to be believed, Travis Walton or Philip Klass?

Consider NICAP's judgment after evaluating the Klass report ("Walton Abduction Cover-Up Revealed"): ". . . it seems that the indications are that a hoax has been perpetrated. . . ."

Big-name TV shows did skits about the ludicrous UFO kidnapping claim in the Arizona woods.

Ponderous talk-show pundits sneered cleverly down their long noses while expostulating about the entire affair.

News accounts of the Walton case all but vanished in the aftermath of the Klass revelations.

The once-great debate seemed finally dead. The Klass report alone did not do it in, but it seemed to be the last definitive word on the incredible bewildering maze of events. But the Klass report was badly flawed, by both its errors and omissions—factors not unknown to his evolution as a UFO expert.

In 1966, Klass was a highly regarded writer and editor for *Aviation Week and Space Technology*, a rather prestigious and often esoteric aeronautical trade journal. Informed that a scientific organization to which he belonged was preparing to hold a symposium on UFOs, Klass protested furiously. The subject, he complained bitterly, was beneath himself, the organization, and science in general.

He proposed that the symposium be junked. Instead, he was invited to participate in the full airing of conflicting views about UFOs. Unhappily, he realized, he didn't know anything about them, had no interest in them, and had long ago put them down to hoax and delusion.

Now, he decided, suddenly joined to battle with them, he'd better at least read a recent book about them. A friend recommended *Incident at Exeter,* written by renowned author-journalist John Fuller. The book carefully documented mass UFO sightings in and around Exeter, New Hampshire, during 1965. Many of the sightings seemed to have occurred near high-tension power lines.

Klass began reading, positive that he could blow holes in all the eyewitness reports, thereby destroying the credibility of the UFO stories so he could easily attribute them to hoax and delusion—his preconceived theory.

The eyewitness stories, however, held up. There were too many, and they were corroborated too often by other independent witnesses. People had seen masses of unidentified flying objects. However, Klass decided, they were not objects at all—they were freaks of electrical nature, globs of charged-up atmosphere, electrified plasmas.

And what exactly was such a plasma, what caused it, and how was it made? Klass didn't know. He could not even define the fundamental term "plasma." He figured that he'd better do some homework before springing this monumental discovery on his learned confreres. So he set about gathering evidence to prove his conclusion.

Plasmas were an oddball family of atmospheric phenomena. They might be created from ball lightning, high-tension power lines, masses of ionized air saturated with pollutants and energized by any number of electrical sources, or even radio and TV signals. Theoretically, the plasmic blobs of electrified air might act just like UFOs—they would hover in neutralized areas; they would seem to chase objects composed of opposite polar charges; they would shoot away from objects charged with like polarity; they would fly erratically in reaction to natural electromagnetic fields; they would seem to change size, shape, speed, and direction, as though they were under intelligent control. But all the while they would actually be controlled by surrounding atmospheric conditions. So they would disrupt electrical systems in cars and homes; they would appear to be objects to the naked eye and also to tracking radar, and they would suddenly disappear (seemingly at tremendous speeds) once their energy was dissipated and dissolve into the surrounding air.

That was the theory. But the chasm between the theory and verifiable evidence was enormous. The fact was that the true nature of plasmas was almost as mysterious as the nature of UFOs themselves. Thus, one mystery was offered to explain another. And the theory faltered badly when confronted by the exact incidents reported by reliable and rational people whose face-to-face experiences with UFOs thoroughly contradicted the plasma explanation. Klass therefore summarily decided that the judgment of these people was faulty. His method of dealing with their evidence was harsh, smug, superior, unfair, and sometimes worse. And when push came to shove, and evidence could not be impugned, Klass simply ignored it and omitted it from consideration.

So his investigation of UFOs finally suffered from several interrelated defects: there was a personal taint of obnoxia about it; it failed to deal with the complete subject; its conclusion was no more substantial than the premise that had spawned it.

Nonetheless, Klass declared, UFOs were mostly electrical freaks. The rest were born of hoax, delusion, mistaken identity, and whatnot. True, the mystery of plasmas themselves was so great that they could not be completely identified and described. Still, if UFOs were not the result of ball lightning, power-line corona, or electrified masses of ionized air, then they were something very much like those freaks of nature. The mystery of UFOs, Klass finally deduced, was easily explained by the equally mysterious atmospheric plasmas.

Thus did he "identify" UFOs in his first book as an expert, from which he launched his new career of "proving" that manned spacecraft from other worlds do not exist.

However, during a 1968 Congressional inquiry into UFOs, the Klass theory was roundly scoured by a host of eminent scientists called to testify. Among them was Dr. James E. McDonald, who at forty was the senior physicist at the University of Arizona's Institute of Atmospheric Physics and one of the nation's genuine experts in the field from which Klass had devised his theory.

McDonald had been skeptical about UFOs until he embarked on an intensive investigation, interviewing hundreds of eyewitnesses to apparently valid encounters. Aside from people who honestly misidentify natural phenomena, he told the congressmen, there is something else going on in the skies, and it has been reliably reported by people all over the world.

"We must very quickly have very good people looking into this problem, because it appears to be one of very serious concern. We are dealing here with inexplicable phenomena, baffling phenomena, that will not be clarified by any but the best scientists. General Samford, of the air force, when he was director of Intelligence, put it very well: 'Credible observers are observing relatively incredible objects.' There is an impressive core of consistency [to the worldwide stories]. Everybody is talking about an object, not hazy lights, that has no wings. All of ten people who saw it may say it was dome-shaped, or something like that . . . but predominently they are disc-shaped objects, elongated cigar-shaped objects, objects without wings, without appendages, without tails, without evident means of propulsion . . . hovering, stopping cars, sometimes soundless, sometimes making humming sounds. There is a tendency for the UFO witness not to think that he is looking at a spaceship, but rather it must be an ambulance out there with a blinking red light, or that it is a helicopter. . . . Then he realizes that the thing is stopped in mid-air, and it is going backward, and it has six bright lights, or something like that. . . . [Finally] you have a feeling that you are dealing with some very high technology, devices of an entirely real nature that defy explanation in terms of present-day science. To say that we could

176

anticipate the values, reasons, motivations, and so on of such a system that has the capability of getting here from somewhere else is fallacious."

McDonald detailed a long list of cases in which many observers all observed the same incredible event at the same time—whole towns, a missionary group, both the audience and professional performers at an air show, journalists, and commercial pilots.

In Redlands, California, dogs started barking all over town one night. People went outside to see what was going on. A disc was hovering over the streets. Hundreds of people watched it streak skyward. It stopped, hovered again, and revealed jet-like openings in its belly. Then it shot off and disappeared in an incredible burst of speed.

In New Guinea, Anglican missionary Reverend William B. Gill and three dozen school workers watched a bright disc descend from an early evening sky. Figures appeared on a deck near the top of the disc. A blue spotlight flashed on and off as the figures seemed to toil with some task on the deck. The witnesses waved; the figures waved back. One of the missionaries signaled with a flashlight; the object seemed to answer back with a pendulum-like swing of its body.

During an air show at Longview, Washington, three discs flew into the middle of a sky-writing exhibition. A former navy commander, manning the public address system, announced the sudden presence of the intruders. For nearly half an hour, pilots, engineers, policemen, and citizens all watched the objects hover, flutter, and fly off at a terrific speed in the broad daylight of a stormless day.

Eight staff members of the American Newspaper Publishers Association watched a UFO hover at the UN building, in the middle of New York City. It was cushion-shaped, wingless, soundless, and it rocked to and fro as it glowed orange, blinking a white light on and off. Abruptly, it rose straight up and took off at a tremendous speed, quickly disappearing.

A mass of objects maneuvered over Farmington, New Mexico, in full view of the whole town. An air force investigation reported that the residents had been watching Skyhook balloons. McDonald investigated the air force claim. He discovered that no Skyhook balloons had been released anywhere in the United States on or close to that day.

In Washington, D.C., both air force and CAA radar tracked "unknowns" moving at from one hundred to eight hundred miles an hour. At the same time, numerous airline pilots reported observing luminous objects flying through the same area. Some of the airliners were vectored into the objects by the CAA radar. Officially, the phenomena were attributed to technical propagations. McDonald checked all the data that had led to the official explanation; the data did not lead to the announced conclusion.

"This was not an explained case," he stated. "It was an instance of unidentified aerial objects flying over our capital."

The Klass theory, he said, "that the really interesting UFOs are atmospheric-electric plasmas of some type similar to ball lightning, but also perhaps something different, something we don't yet understand, but something generated by atmospheric processess," simply is not tenable.

"The first time anyone tried the ball-lightning hypothesis was in the air force's Project Grudge, way back in 1949. The air force position at that time, and since then, was that ball lightning doesn't come near to explaining these sightings. No one ever tried to pursue this theory until Klass began writing about it. There is little enough scientific information to back up his contentions. Klass has ignored most of what is known about ball lightning, and most of what is known about plasmas, and also most of what is known about interesting UFOs.

"When you deal with multiple-witness cases involving discs with metallic luster, definite outline, seen in the daytime, completely removed from a thunderstorm, perhaps seen toward the center of Manhattan, or Redlands, California, they are not ball lightning or plasmas. In weather completely unrelated to anything that could provide a source of energy to maintain a plasma, Klass' views just do not make good sense. It is just not reasonable to suggest that, say, the BOAC Stratocruiser that was followed by six UFOs for ninety miles up in the St. Lawrence Valley was followed by a plasma, or that people in

Redlands were looking at a plasma, or that the twenty or so objects that went over Farmington were plasmas. One of the most characteristic features of plasma is its very short lifetime, microseconds."

Long before Klass appeared on the UFO scene, Mc-Donald said, laboratory scientists had succeeded in creating plasmas in vacuums, energizing them with artificial power. "And still, the difficulty of sustaining a plasma for more than microseconds is a very great difficulty. To suggest that clear weather conditions can somehow create and maintain plasmas that persist for many minutes, and fool pilots with eighteen thousand flight hours into thinking that they [the plasmas] are white- and red-domed discs, to take a very famous case over Philadelphia where the pilot thought he was about one hundred yards from the domed disc, is unreasonable. It is not a scientifically well-defended viewpoint."

Klass did not resurrect the plasma theory for the Walton case. His theory was simply that the Walton story was a hoax. But his method of investigation and the quality of his evidence were not very much improved. Upon close scrutiny, Klass was still stuck with an ill-defended viewpoint.

Close scrutiny, however, was not generally applied to his thesis. And a certain truth finally emerged, though it did not seem to dawn on anyone but the Waltons. While they were accused of being rabid UFO buffs who had perpetrated a hoax to make some money, it was actually people like Klass who had made a money-making profession out of the entire subject—they were the true UFO buffs, with great personal and financial stake invested in all such stories.

No subject in all the world attracted greater readership than a good solid yarn about UFOs. People like the Waltons were the grist for the commercial publishing mills; people like Klass were the grinders.

All of which did not mean that the hoax-criers were not right. It only meant that not one of them could prove that Travis' story was false, just as he could not prove that his story was true.

The basic problem was: How does anyone prove such a story?

Astronomer Carl Sagan once offered his answer: bring back an artifact from the UFO; the captain's log will do just fine.

But in the absence of foresight, as well as incredible cheek, Travis had returned without an artifact to prove his abduction, if, indeed, he had been abducted.

Which left his dilemma unresolved.

The lie-detector tests might have tended to confirm his tale. But he flunked one; the other was invalid, according to Klass.

So Travis proposed a third. The proposal came in the form of a gauntlet thrown down to Philip Klass—put up, or shut up. Travis and the other six members of Mike Rogers' work crew signed a challenge stating that each of them agreed to take a polygraph test administered by any expert of Klass' choice. If they passed, Klass would pay all expenses; if they failed, he would pay nothing.

Since he was so certain of the hoax, how could he lose?

Oddly enough, Klass equivocated, seeming to agree, then growing cool to the idea. Perhaps he was not so sure of his case, after all.

Unbeknownst to him, and to all the other Walton critics, the *National Enquirer* was not so sure of the case, either. In fact, one day after the McCarthy polygraph test, the newspaper "pulled out," according to Jim Lorenzen, "mainly as a result of Rosenbaum's conclusions. They tried to talk APRO into dropping the case, also."

One immediate casualty was the bag of clothes that Travis had been wearing during his alleged abduction. The clothes had been delivered to the *Enquirer* for complete forensic testing. When the *Enquirer* editors dropped the case, they returned the clothes, which were then thrown into the back of Duane's car and forgotten. They were never tested.

A month after the polygraph test, on December 16, the *Enquirer* published its full report on the Walton case. But it did not mention the crucial McCarthy polygraph test, and in no way did it indicate that the newspaper was withdrawing from the investigation.

Coincidentally, several questions were later raised about the McCarthy test. First, what was McCarthy's attitude toward Travis and the UFO story? Was he subjectively hostile, or objectively neutral?

According to Lorenzen, "When McCarthy showed up for the test he was extremely nervous, chain-smoking and shaking like he had the palsy. I have seen him under other circumstances and know that this is not his characteristic behavior. McCarthy was apparently influenced by press reports [that the abduction was a hoax]. He claimed, during a broadcast in July, 1976, with Travis and I present, that Travis had told him during the pre-test interview that he and his family were UFO buffs. Quite the opposite is true [as recorded] on the tape of that session. McCarthy [on the tape] repeatedly tries to get Travis to own up to having expressed a deep wish to ride on a flying saucer, and Travis keeps denying it. He finally agrees to having thought of it [because he probably had thought of it at some time in the past]. Also in the pre-test interview, McCarthy makes it clear that he does not accept Travis' shook-up condition as real. When Travis is not able to tell him the date, or how long he had been gone, McCarthy snaps, 'Where have you been, in a vacuum?' "

The language and tone of the McCarthy report itself was a tip-off that the examiner was apparently not exactly neutral toward his subject. Thus, McCarthy reported: "It was obvious during the examination that he was deliberately attempting to distort his respiration pattern." That is, Travis' breathing seemed to pause at irregular intervals, not especially often, but noticeably enough.

The question was: Did the pause indicate attempted deception, or was it a natural habit, perhaps even a medically related symptom?

As it happened, several interviewers noticed the respiration quirk when Travis was not undergoing lie-detection examination. In certain situations during which Travis was talking for long periods of time, he would suddenly appear to stop breathing for several seconds.

Jim Lorenzen observed: "I have [also] noticed the respiration pause that Travis has. I have one, too, more pronounced if I'm nervous. It's as though I forget to breathe."

McCarthy made no inquiry into any possible alternative reason for this breathing quirk in Travis. He immediately adjudged it to be a deliberate attempt to defraud. And perhaps it was. But a year after Travis was unhooked from McCarthy's polygraph machine, he was still doing it.

15.

JUST LIKE PHILIP KLASS, DR. HYNEK HAD ONCE CON-
sidered the entire subject of UFOs "rank nonsense." For
more than twenty years, he had served as a top consultant to the air force studies of the phenomena, and he
was the expert who had once attributed a massive wave
of Michigan sightings to swamp gas. So much derision
was heaped upon his theory that he decided to attack
the whole subject head-on.

He set about to personally investigate the most baffling cases, those "reports of aerial phenomena that continued to defy explanation in conventional scientific
terms." He was almost certain that when he talked to
the witnesses face to face, he would find them flawed—
the answer was in the observer, and not in the events
observed.

Instead, he found that he was wrong. Again and
again he came face to face with people who told him
stories about their seemingly unbelievable encounters
with unidentified flying objects. They were perfectly reliable people reporting responsible observations. Only the
events that they described were incredible.

He finally concluded: "The UFO phenomenon does
not seem to fit into the established scientific world; it
seems to flaunt itself before our present-day science."

Thus, he told the House Committee of Science and
Astronautics: "When one or more obviously reliable persons report—as has happened many times—that a
brightly illuminated object hovered a few hundred feet
above their automobile, and that during that incident

their car motor stopped, the headlights dimmed or went out, and the radio stopped playing, only to have these functions return to normal after the disappearance of the UFO . . . by what right can we summarily ignore their testimony and imply that they are deluded or just plain liars? When reports of bizarre happenings are verified, when the observers are many and they are responsible, perhaps even reluctant to state what they saw, fearing ridicule . . . then clearly we should pay attention. Something very important may be going on. Can we afford not to look toward the UFO skies? Can we afford to overlook a potential breakthrough of great significance? And even apart from that, the public is growing impatient. The public does not want another twenty years of UFO confusion. They want to know whether there really is something to this whole UFO business. And I can tell you [congressmen] definitely that they are not satisfied with the answers they have been getting. They have an uncanny way of distinguishing between an honest scientific approach and the method of ridicule and persiflage [that usually characterizes official UFO investigations]. The reporters of the truly baffling UFOs are most frequently disinterested or even skeptical people. They are people who are taken by surprise by an experience that they cannot understand."

Dr. McDonald told the congressmen what these surprised people were seeing: "They appear to be craft-like, machine-like devices [corroborated by] a very large body of impressive witnesses' testimony, radar-tracking data on ultra high-speed objects moving at over five thousand miles per hour, combined radar and visual sightings, and just too much other consistent evidence that suggests we are dealing with machine-like devices from somewhere else. The possibility that the earth might be under surveillance by some high civilization in command of technology far beyond ours must not be over-looked in weighing the UFO problem.

"I am one of those who lean toward the extraterrestrial hypothesis. But my scientific instincts lead me to hedge just to the extent of suggesting that if the UFOs are not of extra-mundane origin, then I suspect that they will prove to be something very much more bizarre, something of perhaps even greater scientific interest than extraterrestrial devices. The recurrent observations by reliable citizens here and abroad over the past twenty-five years cannot be brushed aside as nonsense, but rather need to be taken extremely seriously as evidence that some phenomenon is going on that we simply do not understand."

"Can there really be intelligent life out there?" the congressmen asked.

Dr. Carl Sagan answered: "I have enough difficulty trying to determine if there is intelligent life on earth to be sure if there is intelligent life anywhere else. . . . Nonetheless, the number of suns in our galaxy is about 150,000,000,000. Now, in a collection of 150,000,000,000 stars in the Milky Way Galaxy our sun, is just one, and there are at least billions of other galaxies, each of which contain about 100,000,000,000 stars, as well. So it is clear that there are in the accessible universe some hundreds of billions of billions of stars, all more or less like our own. It turns out that at least the molecules fundamental to living systems are produced relatively easily, the physics and chemistry apparently made in such a way that origin of life may be a likely event. If civilizations tend to have very long lifetimes, it may be that there are large numbers of technical civilizations in the galaxy. If there are other civilizations, many of them are likely to be far in advance of our own, and this, therefore, raises the question of how likely it is that they can traverse interstellar space and come from planets or some other star to here. There is nothing in the physics that prohibits interstellar space flight. . . ."

How could it be done?

Dr. Harder explained: "Concerning the propulsion of UFOs, a tentative hypothesis would be that it is connected with an application of gravitational fields that we do not understand. There are theoretical grounds for believing that there must exist a second gravitational field, corresponding to the magnetic field in electromagnetic theory, the basis for our modern electrical generators and motors. Someday, perhaps, we will learn enough to apply gravitational forces in the same way that we have learned to apply electromagnetic forces.

"The spacecraft itself would have to be built to withstand tremendous pressures, to deal with stress on materials beyond our present-day technology."

Harder revealed that Brazilian fishermen near the coastal town of Ubatuba reported watching a flying saucer explode in flight, dropping flaming debris just offshore. The fishermen claimed to have recovered some of the debris. Examined by the Brazilian Mineral Production Laboratory, the metal tested out to be pure magnesium, apparently devoid of any alloys. Totally pure metals are metals possessed of extreme strength, free of imperfections in their crystal structure. Spectographic and X-ray diffraction upheld the first analysis—pure magnesium, even without impurities that might be expected to be traced in during the manufacturing process. Finally, the materials were placed under neutron activation analysis. It revealed a one-tenth-of-one-percent deviation from perfect purity.

The alleged UFO debris was barely traced with zinc, barium, and strontium. If it had come from a crashed spaceship, its strength could be computed at millions of pounds per square inch—perfectly capable of withstanding the stresses inherent to the impossible maneuverings attributed to streaking UFOs.

"We can well imagine," Dr. Harder said, "that such a high purity crystal, free of surface and internal imperfections, would achieve fantastic strengths."

"If spaceships from other worlds were actually flying around our skies, wouldn't our sophisticated tracking systems disclose their presence?" the congressmen wanted to know.

No, answered Dr. Robert Baker, a veteran government and industry specialist in astronomy, astronautics, and engineering: those systems are selectively programmed to track only known objects, the ones they are supposed to be tracking; they disregard all others.

"There is only one surveillance system known to me that exhibits sufficient and continuous coverage to have even a slight opportunity of betraying the presence of [UFOs] operating above the earth's atmosphere. The system is classified. But since it has been in operation, there have been a number of anomalistic alarms . . . unexplained on the basis of natural phenomena, interference, equipment malfunction, or man-made space objects. We have not now been, nor have we been in the past, able to achieve a complete, or even partially complete, surveillance of space in the vicinity of earth, comprehensive enough to betray the presence of, or provide quantitative information on, anomalistic phenomena [UFOs]."

The air force and the National Academy of Sciences had long before been charged with the responsibility of resolving the primary question posed about UFOs: What, if anything, were they?

Typical of such governmental investigations was the Condon Report. After several years of intense, case-by-case examination, the Condon Report finally concluded that there was nothing at all to UFOs; they merited no further study.

But within the materials upon which that conclusion had been based were scores of cases that should have led to exactly the opposite conclusion. The research investigators alluded to "the presence of strange vehicles . . . flying objects that must be considered unknowns . . . the probability that at least one genuine UFO was involved . . . the apparently rational, intelligent behavior of the UFO suggests a mechanical device of unknown origin as the most probable explanation of this sighting . . . one of the most puzzling radar cases on record . . . a sighting so rare that it apparently has never been reported before, or since . . . must certainly be classed as an unknown . . . this sighting defies explanation by conventional means . . . cases from the radar-visual files that have no plausible explanation. . . ."

There was photo evidence corroborating "the assertion that an extraordinary flying object—silvery, metallic, disc-shaped, tens of meters in diameter, and evidently artificial —flew within sight of two witnesses."

And "there are three sightings made by the astronauts while in orbit that have not been adequately explained. These are:

1). Gemini Four astronaut McDivitt—observation of a cylindrical object with a protuberance.

2). Gemini Four astronaut McDivitt—observation of a moving bright light at a higher level than the Gemini spacecraft.

3). Gemini Seven astronaut Borman saw what he referred to as a "Bogey" flying in formation with his space-craft.

"The training and perspicacity of the astronauts put their reports of sightings in the highest category of credibility. The three unexplained sightings are a challenge to the analyst. . . ."

As for the sightings closer to earth, they were consistent with the theory that "unknown and extraordinary aircraft have penetrated the air space of the United States."

Which would seem to make them of concern to the government of the United States.

The Condon Report also provided a prime example of why the government was finally hooted out of the UFO business. In a confidential staff memo, the project's intended direction was outlined:

> The trick would be, I think, to describe the project so that, to the public, it would appear to be a totally objective study—but, to the scientific community, it would present the image of a group of nonbelievers trying their best to be objective, but having an almost zero expectation of finding a saucer. . . . We could [therefore] carry off the job to our benefit. . . .

The final benefit of such bureaucratic deceits was that the American people eventually distrusted every governmental pronouncement concerning UFOs. Now the government no longer denies the existence of UFOs. In fact, in 1973, Houston Control tacitly admitted their existence: "They pose no hostile threat to the United States."

So the government is not really out of the UFO business. Its concern has merely become invisible, covert; it has gone underground.

Thus, no official federal interest was discernible in the Travis Walton case. Rumors claimed that FBI agents had been assigned to investigate the alleged abduction by an alien spacecraft. But no federal investigators interviewed Travis Walton or any of the witnesses—at least none who were identified as representatives of the American government. There was some suspicion that government agents had, indeed, taken a close look at the case, but working undercover, disguised as legitimate investigators in order to preserve the government's anonymous interest in such affairs.

Travis Walton thought it was absurd that the government would not make some investigation: "Even if it was a hoax, like so many people say, how could the government know without investigating? And if it wasn't a hoax, and it isn't, shouldn't the government know about it?"

The answer would seem to be yes.

And, after all, national polls indicate that 100,000,000 Americans share an interest in the mystery of the skies— UFO buffs of about equal degree to the Waltons. Some 15,000,000 Americans claim to have seen them. One of them happens to be the president of the United States, Jimmy Carter.

Amidst a massive wave of sightings throughout the South in 1973, Carter refused to ridicule the reports of UFOs or the people who were making them. He was then governor of Georgia and was questioned about a rash of UFO encounters in his state, especially in and around the Hunter Air Base, near Savannah.

Did he believe the reports were legitimate, or a joke?

"I don't laugh at anybody anymore when they say they've seen UFOs," he said, "because I've seen one myself."

Carter said that he and a group of friends were coming out of a dinner meeting one night when something attracted their attention in the blackened sky. They all looked up. There was a big shining light, shaped like a saucer, and hovering soundlessly over their heads.

Carter did not know what it was. It was unidentified, it was flying, and it appeared to be an object, a UFO. It hovered for several moments, glowing, and then it rose silently and sped away, disappearing in a flash.

The future president of the United States thereby became one of those legions of seemingly reliable people who had reported observing an incredible event . . . one of those people whom Congress had been advised not to ignore or dismiss summarily as deluded or just plain liars.

And Carter's credentials were all the more impressive because he was also a former naval officer and a scientist, a nuclear physicist—not a man likely to be mistaken by what he had seen with his own eyes.

He had seen evidence of what Dr. McDonald called

"the possibility that the earth might be under surveillance by some high civilization in command of technology far beyond ours."

That is precisely what U.S. Air Force Sergeant Charles Moody claimed was happening, seemingly corroborated by the Travis Walton case.

But was the Moody story true?

Was the Walton story true?

Theoretically, both stories could have been true. Therefore, they should have been of interest to all mankind. Their potential significance was at least as great as anything ever recorded in humanity's history. In fact, their import, if true, imperiled many of mankind's hallowed and fundamental beliefs and concepts inscribed in history —ideas concerning life, its origins, divinity, infinity, time, space, dimension . . . perhaps the whole meaning of the human existence, and its final destiny.

The United States expended about $16,000,000,-000 a year on its intelligence-gathering agencies. The government spent millions of dollars to find out why children fell off tricycles, to research why monkeys clench their jaws, why people fall in love, to teach mothers how to play with their children, to study Indo-Australian ants, Central American toads, Yugoslavian lizards, Polish frogs, Aboriginal sweat smells, the "goodness of fit" between psychological orientations of individuals and the sociocultural matrix in Nepal. In 1977, NASA requested $2,800,-000 just to build a house for one hundred pounds of moon rocks.

But the government did not show any overt interest in the possible ramifications of either the Walton or the Moody case, except that Sergeant Moody got transferred overseas. As for the Walton case, many people had been led to believe that on its surface it was outrageously bizarre, unthinkable, not believable. It had been roundly labeled as a hoax, maybe a psychotic delusion, really not worth bothering about by serious-minded people, whose efforts were better directed toward more rational and worthwhile pursuits.

Besides, nobody in all the massive bureaucracy of the federal government was specifically charged with the expressed responsibility for even reviewing the content of such cases. While there were millions of federal jobs assigned for governmental attention to everything from soup to nuts, not one was designated to monitor possibly legitimate and valid UFO cases.

Therefore, if the Travis Walton story was true, the government of the United States might very well be the last to know—a circumstance rather bizarre in itself, but possibly not without some redeeming value.

Meanwhile, some scientists, like Drs. Hynek and Harder, were taking the Walton story, and its possible ramifications, rather seriously. And in both the United States and Russia, other scientists were achieving breakthroughs with experiments that smacked of UFology's concepts.

UFologists had theorized that alien spaceships might be powered by some combination of technology that harnessed gravity, magnetism, and nuclear fusion—the power of the sun.

At the Massachusettes Institute of Technology, researchers created a fuel of plasma fusion, bottled it by manipulation of super-powerful magnetic fields, and contained it in an engine reactor at an incredible temperature of 10,000,000 degrees centigrade—one-fourth the amount required for a full power-producing machine.

The critical remaining problem was to devise a metal so strong that it would withstand the heat and contain the fiery plasma safely.

The crude prototype of an anti-gravity motor had already been demonstrated by a British scientist, Eric Laithwaite, professor of heavy electrical engineering at London's Imperial College of Science and Technology.

Using a system of gyroscopes, normally used to guide spacecraft, Laithwaite reduced the weight of a "power box" by one-fourth—the first step, theoretically, toward achieving total weightlessness, in defiance of gravity. Eventually, Laithwaite claimed, an anti-gravity motor, powered by a pea-sized chunk of nuclear fuel, would fly manned spaceships on extended journeys to the most distant stars.

Which is what UFologists believed had been happening all along—except, they believed, the spaceships were traveling in the opposite direction, from the most distant stars to earth.

To some, the Travis Walton case loomed as one of the

strongest links in the chain of evidence binding together their belief that alien civilizations were, indeed, carefully observing mankind and its tiny planet. Why, they didn't know, nor could they speculate. But, like Dr. Hynek, they thought that "clearly we should pay attention. Something very important may be going on."

1978 . . .

Silently, a tiny speck rushes through the vast black sea that is the sky. The speck is a UFO on a journey from the planet Earth. It is unmanned, a robot probe whose beat of life is sustained by computerized nuclear pulsations as it streaks through yielding space, across the icy galaxy, vaulting into the universe toward the eternity and infinity that stretch beyond the constellations of the Zodiac.

The UFO is Voyager Two. Perhaps still unseen from beyond, it now traverses the glittery Milky Way—100,-000,000,000 stars that rotate in the solar system that is mankind's home. The spaceship aims for the outer reaches of that solar system as it courses past planets, moons, asteroids, comets, meteoroids, rushing across the deep, darkling, showery wash that is the cosmic sea. The spaceship carries a message.

The message is inscribed on a twelve-inch, gold-plated copper disk; it is being sent by the government of one of Earth's troubled nations, the United States. Jimmy Carter, the leader of that nation, says in the message that Earth's people are dispatching the message to anyone, or anything, that may be out there to receive and understand it.

"It is a token of our sounds, our science, our images, our music, our thoughts, and our feelings," the president says. "We are attempting to survive our time so that we may live in yours. We hope someday, having solved the problems that we face, to join the community of galactic civilizations."

The message extends greetings in fifty-five of Earth's languages.

And it portrays the world of man with the sounds of a human kiss, *Beethoven's Fifth Symphony*, singing humpbacked whales, a volcano burbling to eruption, a train whistle, laughter, a cricket clicketing, and the night chant of the Navajo Indians.

The record is also inscribed with a series of code signals that can be translated into the sights of man's world: a baby nursing at its mother's breast, the Great Wall of China, a supermarket, human sex organs, a forest, and a snowflake.

The message is two hours long. Sealed within the natural vacuum of space and its own aluminum jacket, it can remain intact for 1,000,000,000 years. Who, or what, will ever receive it—washed up on some distant planetary shore, perhaps a thousand or more years from now—is not known. Renowned astronomer-biologist Carl Sagan conceived of the message as "launching a bottle into the cosmic ocean" in hopes that some intelligent being from afar might pluck it out and send an answer back to Earth.

Is such communication really possible? Yes, Sagan believes, because "the idea of extraterrestrial life is an idea whose time has come."

These are exactly the sentiments of Russian researcher Vyacheslav Zaitsev, who has spent thirty years documenting what he claims is evidence that intelligent beings from outer space have already made many contacts with Earth. Mankind, he believes, has either ignored the contacts, or simply has not understood them.

From one of his most puzzling cases, Zaitsev theorizes that extraterrestrials may even have landed colonies on Earth. In the rugged Bayan-Kara-Ula mountain range, which borders China and Tibet, cave explorers discovered 716 stone-like discs and a plot of ancient graves.

The discs were etched with spiraled grooves emanating from center holes. Asian wits dubbed them Stone Age gramophone records. But scholars were unable to determine their origin or purpose. Carbon dating placed their age at about twelve thousand years old. Laboratory examination of their composition revealed a curious metal content, especially cobalt. When scraped free of surface particles, the discs vibrated "as if they carried an electric charge," Zaitsev reported, "though it is probably something utterly unknown to us." He, along with other scientists, speculated that the discs were actually inscribed with some form of ancient, or alien, writing that has since defied all attempts to decipher it.

Meanwhile, Chinese archaeologists dug into the graves found near the cache of discs. They discovered vestige skeletons whose age was also dated to twelve thousand years ago. The vestiges indicated a basically humanoid form, and the Chinese somewhat quickly decided that they had uncovered the burial ground of an extinct species of ape.

To which Zaitsev wryly replied: "So far as is known, apes do not bury each other in graves, nor do they write hieroglyphic symbols on stone discs." And he pointedly reminded the Chinese of one of their own most persistent and enduring legends that tells of "small, gaunt, yellow-faced spirit men who came down from the clouds many centuries ago," in the Bayan-Kara-Ula mountains.

Who were they? Where did they come from? What was their purpose?

Zaitsev doesn't know. He suspects that they were a probe colony from outer space. But beyond legend and speculation, none of the massive scientific testing and none of the intense archaeological-anthropological examination have been able to explain the mystery of the stone discs—what they are, where they came from, or why they were stored in the Bayan-Kara-Ula caves near the equally mysterious and baffling ancient burial ground of an unknown life form that left message-like artifacts behind itself.

British astronomer Duncan Lunan agreed completely with Zaitsev's primary postulation: man's Voyager message is not the first to have been transmitted across the galactic sea. And they are far from alone in the scientific community with their shared belief that the messages have been coming from the other direction, from outer space to earth.

Lunan claims that one of those messages is still being broadcast, through an interplanetary satellite 170,000 miles from Earth. That, he is convinced, is the explanation for a series of mysterious radio echoes, first discovered penetrating the atmosphere in the 1920s and never traced to any earthly source.

In a studious research paper published by the highly respected British Interplanetary Society, Lunan concluded that the intermittent radio signals were a message sent to Earth from another solar system, relayed through an unmanned robot probe placed in undetected orbit around Earth's moon about 11,000 B.C.

Lunan plotted the signals on a graph, and the resulting outline depicts the known constellations in their approximate positions during that distant time. From a series of dots that resembles no known constellation, he deciphered the alleged space probe's message:

> Start here. Our home is Upsilon Bootis, which is a double star. We live on the sixth planet of seven. Check that—the sixth of seven, counting outward from the sun, which is the larger of the two. Our sixth planet has one moon. Our fourth planet has three. Our first and third planets each have one. Our probe is in the position of Arcturus, known in our maps.

Upsilon Bootis is about 103,000,000 light-years from Earth. Oddly, on Lunan's graphs, Upsilon Bootis stands strangely out of its correct position—either outright error, or an intended symbol of punctuated emphasis.

After examining Lunan's research, other scientists were not eager to deride it. They believed the calculations and graphs were impressive. Though perhaps not totally accurate by strict astronomical standards. Astronomy recognizes the increasing fallibility of many of its long-cherished dictates.

One of America's leading radio astronomers, Professor Ronald Bracewell, of Stanford University, had been exchanging research material with Lunan for years, and he found him to be a sound and perceptive scientist. Bracewell himself had done similar work on the radio echoes, but he came to no solid conclusions about their source or meaning.

He refused to dismiss the Lunan thesis as nonsense, pointing out that the radio signals are real, they appear to come from somewhere in space, and theoretically they could be coming from a robot satellite near Earth's moon.

"The echoes exist," Bracewell emphasized. "When one plots them as Lunan did, one gets a very very curious result. There is something uncanny about it. But it's in the interpretation of them that one lets one's hair down. It could mean many things. It may be a message, or it may not be a message at all. We simply don't know."

Nor might extraterrestrials know what Voyager's twelve-inch disc is supposed to be or how to play it on a phonographic turntable at 16 2/3 revolutions per minute or how to decipher the coded photographic images—even assuming that they will have ears to hear and eyes to see the message that Earth sends to them.

Mankind is just now in the process of discovering how little it really does know about the fathomless void beyond its own small world. No longer is the Earth the center of the universe, nor the sun, nor even man's galaxy. Many solid and absolute facts of the past are being startled into discredit by new discovery. The four moons once ascribed to Jupiter by Galileo are now known to be at least thirteen. Science has become very uncertain about what does exist beyond its earthly grasp. It is in the "Columbus stage" of exploration sailing forth across that immense galactic frontier.

Thus, in 1977, a "new" disc-shaped star was discovered in the constellation Cygnus, about 10,000 light-years from Earth. The flat, luminous presence is ten times the size of Earth's sun, thirty times its mass. Its fiery glow is masked by a circling band of non-luminous gas in which outer planets may exist. And its fundamental telescopic image is not basically dissimilar from Earth's, if Earth were viewed from there.

In the center of that same constellation, scientists believe, mysterious black holes exist—massive stars exhausted of their nuclear energy, so they implode, collapsing inward on themselves, becoming so dense that no light can escape their own gravitational pull. Thus, they become the size of ordinary planets: unseen, unknown, not necessarily devoid of life.

In late 1977, the Naval Research Laboratory announced that its new detection satellite, orbiting two hundred thirty miles above Earth, may have discovered one of these invisible stars.

Near the center of the constellation Circinus, where no known star exists, something was generating bursts of X-rays. The only measurable evidence of a black hole's existence would be the X-ray bursts generated when its tremendous gravity drew gas from nearby space at such speed as to heat the gas to millions of degrees of temperature.

The science of the universe is just trembling at the brink of this cosmic frontier. And already it is being asked: Could life exist on these invisible stars or on some other shore of this uncharted and unexplored gulf?

Well, the definition of life itself has suddenly, starkly expanded beyond the certitude of its ancient confines. Long ago, science had determined that there were only two kinds of life on Earth: the higher forms—animals and plants; the lower forms—bacteria.

That knowledge was safe, certain, and immutable— until very late in 1977, when the National Science Foundation and NASA made a startling announcement. A University of Illinois research team had discovered a "new" form of life, one that dated backward to the earliest period of Earth's formation, billions of years ago, when the environment of Earth's surface was probably very much like the environments of some distant planets.

The "new" form of life was a tiny organism previously classified as bacteria. But by manipulating the newly aborning knowledge of genetics, the researchers had discovered its completely separate and distinctive characteristics.

"It is a new form of life on this planet," they announced. It lived without oxygen, in tremendous heat, and it produced methane gas—sometimes called swamp gas. One of its favorite abodes was the stomachs of cows.

The researchers were well nigh overwhelmed by one possible ramification of the discovery: the possibility that the organism was a clue to life forms that had evolved elsewhere, not only elsewhere in Earth's solar system, but beyond in the deeper universe.

Extraterrestrial life was not only an idea whose time had come, they agreed, but it was an idea probably substantiated by their astounding discovery. The organism could very well be the basic building block for life on other planets. So the find, in their judgment, increased enormously the chances that extraterrestrial life did exist. The odds had suddenly multiplied incredibly. Now, in fact, it seemed likely to them that some form of life had to exist on other planets; it would be almost incredible if it did not.

Dr. Richard Young, chief of NASA's planetary biology section, stated: "To find extraterrestrial life, we must now start looking at a much broader range of conditions. What we are facing here is an utterly new concept of how life evolves. The ultimate ramifications may be staggering to everything we have believed to date about the origins of life and where it may exist."

So the mind of science is changing about many things. And the idea of UFOs is no longer anathema to its purist creed. Dissipation of its long-standing scorn and contempt was manifested in a recent confidential survey of 2,611 members of the no-nonsense American Astronomical Society. In an unusually high rate of response, fifty-two percent, the scientists checked off queries about their views on UFOs: fifty-three percent said that UFOs were worthy of further study; seventy-five percent said they were receptive to serious documentation.

Considering the full range of changed attitude, Dr. Hynek noted: "People are beginning to recognize that there are serious aspects to this phenomena, that trivial solutions like 'meteorological effects' no longer wash. The scientific party line on UFOs has always been: 'If you can't put it into an equation, to hell with it.' But UFOs just haven't gone away. They haven't been a fad. On the contrary, reports of sightings are on the increase. It's a case of the scientists following the lead of the public in wanting to know what they are, what is going on."

The president of the United States has even expressed his belief that the time has come to seriously address the issue and resolve it. And in the United Nations, Sir Eric Gairy, prime minister of Grenada, has formally asked the world body to undertake a complete investigation of worldwide UFO reports—especially to determine if the unidentified flying objects might ultimately pose a hostile threat to man.

That is a possibility that Czech-British astronomer Zdenek Kopal views with some alarm, because "in a confrontation with extraterrestrial beings intelligent enough to have discovered our existence, we might find ourselves in their test tubes, to be investigated as we do guinea pigs."

The implication inherent to all the so-called UFO abduction cases is that the human victims were examined like guinea pigs by their alien captors. It is a recurring circumstance, repeated in each and every chronicled case—from Betty and Barney Hill, to Charlie Hickson and Calvin Parker, who were allegedly taken from a Pascagoula fishing dock, through a handful of lesser known cases, to Travis Walton. But in no instance was hostility expressed toward any of the alleged victims—not by their alien abductors, anyway.

Perhaps it is all just fantasy, psychosis, or hoax; perhaps not.

The final answer to the primary question is that the final answer is not known. In pursuit of knowledge, sound minds are simply asked to suspend judgment; gather the evidence, sift it, analyze it, test, ruminate, wonder, search for the answer. The Old-World way of automatic, knee-jerk rejection leads a path through ignorance.

Thus, the world was once flat, the Earth was the center of the universe, God was in His heaven, and all was right with the world. It was a world in which the very idea of Christine Jorgensen could not exist, nor the idea of clones, where Icarus flying was mere legend and not prophecy. Who, then, could have imagined a single bomb that would destroy whole cities and exterminate all their people?

Oddly, however, the idea of UFOs is very old, indeed. Going backward in time, through the writings and carvings and legends of mankind, it is possible to trace the record of sightings, strange flying objects and their mysterious occupants, to approximately 45,000 B.C. The records tell of luminous discs, flying suns, fiery chariots wheeling across the amazed skies, mystical creatures robed in white, and spirit-gods descending from ships of clouds that flew earthward from the sun and the stars and farther beyond. Roman scribes recorded a massive wave of what modern man would call UFOs. Who is modern man to say that they were all deluded, or just plain liars?

As written history became more consistent, so did the sightings—usually described and interpreted in accord with the knowledge and philosophy coincident with the times. But the essential reports were always the same: strange vehicles were maneuvering across the fathomless skies, sometimes landing, sometimes disgorging strange occupants, sometimes departing with human passengers—almost never leaving preserved traces behind.

The records prove nothing. But they do exist. Their meaning is a mystery.

Even as now: March, 21, 1977—police, highway patrolmen, sheriffs' deputies, and citizens all observed brightly lighted objects maneuvering across the darkened California nighttime skies. The objects zoomed, hovered, cruised, sped away from pursuing helicopters, buzzed March Air Force Base in the desert, fifty miles east of Los Angeles, zipped low over Whittier Hills, paused above Box Spring Canyon, and at the same time other lighted objects flew in formation over Firestone, fifty miles to the west. For nine straight hours, UFOs streaked across near-Earth: the Long Beach Airport, Huntington Beach, Ventura, Riverside, San Bernardino—all observed and reported by astonished and responsible people.

Time is a continuum in which UFOs endure and persist.

Travis Walton is married now, to Dana Rogers, Mike's sister. They live in a small apartment above a rug store on Snowflake's modest Main Street. Travis has new responsibilities, bills to pay, and groceries to buy. Children will probably soon start coming along, with more mouths to feed.

For a time, he returned to the woods, trying to labor again at his old craft, trying to feel good about it again. But it didn't work. The woods disturbed him. They had marked him forever on the night of his dreadful voyage, he claimed.

So he did apprentice work in carpentry, did odd jobs, and struggled to deal with his bizarre world, which he swore he never made. He confided: "I'm really getting a bit tired of talking about the whole experience. I would sort of like to forget all that and get on with my life. One of these days I'm going to just close the curtain and walk off. . . . It really doesn't matter to me anymore what people believe."

On the other hand, quite quietly he continued to undergo testing, like voice-stress analysis, still seeking the proof for what he insists really happened to him. With his sardonic gleam of eye, he said he might uncover something important, remember something of great significance under further hypnosis . . . and not tell anyone else about it.

Ridicule and denigration have hardened his mettle, glinted it with cynicism. He was hurt by the shotgunned repudiation of his story. Still not invulnerable, he looked back on the scathing reaction, pondered it: "Everyone seemed to view the story with already-made-up minds. Every investigator tried to explain it only according to his own particular field of expertise, as if nothing else existed in the world."

Thus, the psychiatrist saw it as something in the mind, a passing psychosis, a hallucination (somehow shared by six witnesses, ergo mass hysteria). Dr. Rosenbaum told Travis that the experience was rooted in the deprivations of his fatherless childhood. So the UFO's flashing lights were the flashing lights of his mother's answering-service switchboard (though there was no switchboard, no lights, only a bank of common telephones). That fantasy was connected to his desire for his father to return and take him away (though he never knew his father, never was concerned about him).

The lawman saw the experience in terms of crime—it was a hoax.

The drug expert saw it as a narcotic trip. Therefore, the two-mm red spot near his elbow became a needle puncture, though seemingly an unnecessarily eccentric method of ingesting LSD, and in the wrong arm, too.

The journalist saw it in terms of whatever he had to prove, as in the case of Philip Klass, whose sole and publicly stated interest in UFOs is only to prove that they do not exist.

"The ideal UFO witness," Travis concluded, "in order to be believed, would have to be someone who was never in trouble, never saw anything mystifying before, never thought of UFOs, never spoke of them, never even heard of them at all. Maybe, just maybe, he'd be believed."

So scratch one fifth grader at the Snowflake Elementary School. His teacher noticed that the boy seemed especially sleepy and inattentive in class.

"You're going to have to stop watching television at night," she told him, "and go to bed on time."

"I don't watch television at night," he replied.

"Then why are you so sleepy every day?"

"Because we watch the UFOs from my bedroom window at night. Sometimes they are out there all night long, back by the hills. We watch them fly in and out, up and down. And they go *pffft!* And they disappear. Sometimes we just watch them all night long."

For someone doggedly tracking the events from that long-ago night in November, 1975, it is a wearisome trail, mocking and taunting. What is true? What is false? The hard evidence peters out, the leads, the clues. Months roll up into years. Only the odd bits and pieces remain on the tenuous string.

Travis writes: "Keep digging. There's been a multitude of rumors flying, but I have confidence that you will get to the bottom of each of them. . . . Peace and good luck."

Rumors: before he disappeared, Travis told a woman neighbor that UFOs were after him and were going to kidnap him; Travis once had been involved in a plot to bomb the Snowflake High School; Travis had participated in the burglary of the Snowflake drugstore, and Marshal Flake had found him counting through a pile of stolen pills on the floor of a friend's home.

The rumors were all false.

"Thanks," Travis writes, "for helping correct all the false malicious rumors and errors. It is a far cry from the treatment I have received from some of the other journalists I have encountered. I'm always the last to hear these tales. Hearing something from more than one person in a small town does not make the story more true. It just means the story is more than an hour old."

His moods somersault, from boyish gratefulness to fishwife anger: "Why won't you accept what I tell you? You listen to everybody else. . . . You don't believe a damned thing I say, anyway."

Then fetching remorse: "My anger wasn't really directed at you, but out of justifiable concern, considering my circumstances, all the smears, and false accusations."

The odd bits and pieces trickle in more slowly.

Fred Sylvanus, who does not believe the story, nonetheless writes: "Have some info re: military observatory near here [Phoenix] about UFOs the Walton night. . . ." He cannot obtain confirmation.

Jim Lorenzen writes: "Now, with Travis, we have a philosopher syndrome to deal with. When you ask him if he's telling the truth, he begins to think of truth in an absolute sense and he wonders if he knows the truth, and this is enough to upset the polygraph or P.S.E. [voice-stress examination]. . . . On the control question, 'Were you born in Phoenix?,' Travis says, 'Yes,' and the P.S.E. shows stress. What does this mean? I think it means that Travis worries about anything that he cannot testify to out of his conscious memory. Very few of us can remember our birth. . . ."

And snatching at straws, Lorenzen writes: "There is a possible corroborating witness to Travis' return. In his early account, he remembered someone across the street when he reached the phone booths at Heber; the person just walked away." Two years later, of course, the possible witness could not be found.

Even the rabid attacks by critics dwindle, though Spaulding occasionally fires a sputtering salvo: "This is the biggest hoax ever perpetrated on the American people. I have five hundred pages of documentation to prove it." His documentation makes no distinction between proof and premise.

So it goes. As time piles up, other events of life intrude, and attention directs itself to closer urgencies—a sick child, bursted water pipes, berserk government, the cat hit by a car, soaring prices, and other stories that buy the bread and pay the mortgage. The Walton story recedes in memory, though it still nags and nettles somewhere far back in dim consciousness. It becomes easy to believe that it did not happen. Time and distance from the event allow the tracker to relax back into that old, familiar, comfortable world that existed before. Grown men don't believe that kind of story—too incredible, too bizarre. Where's the proof? Snatched by spacemen from another world? Impossible. Really?

Once the world was flat. . . .

So out come all the tapes again, all the tape recordings of all the people telling their story of suddenly being hurled into just such an impossible event. And it all returns with its first full power and force and credulity— that which does make it believable, utterly, hearing again the voices, the emotion, the guileless awe, sometimes astonishment, as they tell their incredible tale . . . Travis and Mike and John and all the others. They relive it as they speak, step by step, moment by moment, shock by shock.

There is the light in the woods. It's a UFO. Travis jumps out of the truck and runs toward it. The men in the truck scream at him to come back. A beam of light fires out of the bottom of the craft. Travis is slammed backward, head over heels. The others flee. When they return, Travis is gone. But gone where? Aboard the UFO. . . .

They are all credible people, seemingly sincere in their recounting of a thoroughly incredible event. Why should they not be believed?

There is no final answer, though a line from Pope's *Essay on Man* persists in buzzing at the inner ear: "Sole judge of truth, in endless error hurled: the glory, jest, and riddle of the world!" It's not an answer, but a guide.

Of a night, the high Mogollon Plateau fades back into darkness, looking just like the vast and desolate range once roamed by the Apache and Navajo and Hopi, whose most ancient ancestors told of lights in the skies and mysterious spirit creatures who winged their way through the forever skies on engines of clouds that flashed. And sometimes they departed on ships of rock, with human warriors taken from the tribes. Between legend and prophecy, mystery remains on the ancient land.

Overhead, a jetliner passes on its moonlit route, winking down on a lunarscape that is flat and slate-colored, pocked by meteor-like gougings. It has passed over hundreds of vacant desert miles, riveted only by single needle-etched roads that seem to wander aimlessly, but which abruptly sew their solitary seam to a patch of twinkling town. Then comes emptiness again, until the lunarscape upcrops into glacial rock, the broken-back mountains fissured out of pre-history's primordial sea.

And much higher up in the nighttime sky, unseen, two UFOs streak across the vast abrupt of space, Voyagers One and Two, on their mission to the galactic frontier, Earth's deepest probe in its search of new worlds. In time, they will send back their own messages to Earth, as they photograph the moons of Jupiter, slingshot themselves off Jupiter's gravity to soar across the stark expanse to Saturn, photograph its moons and rings, all the while measuring the atmospheric nebulae surrounding both planets—thick, swirling, boiling masses of hydrogen and helium so like the plasm from which the Sun and Earth may have been created.

Glancing backward through the rings of Saturn, the Voyager eyes will see Earth looking just like the flaring soup that other planets appear to be when viewed from Earth. They will take an especially close look at Titan, the largest known satellite in the solar system, whose atmospheric pressure is believed to be similar to Earth's, and whose surface may contain basic life-forming compounds.

As man counts through his calendar of 1981, the Voyagers will rocket farther out through time, to Uranus, then Neptune, rushing even beyond the ecliptic, past Pluto, flung finally into another galaxy—on a silent journey through the billions of miles, across the eons, where time and space comingle eternity with infinity.

And that is still just another brink, for there are billions of galaxies beyond there, billions upon billions upon billions of stars and planets—all the faces of the universe as yet undared, unmet, undisturbed.

They will be the yearnings for tomorrow. . . .

Epilogue

Space may produce new worlds; whereof so rife
There went a rumor in Heaven that He ere long
Intended to create, and therein plant
A generation whom His choice regard
Should favor equal to the sons of Heaven. . . .

. . . whom shall we send
In search of this new world,
Whom shall we find sufficient?
Who shall attempt with wandering feet
The dark, unbottomed, infinite abyss
And through the palpable darkness find out
His unknown way, or spread his aery flight
Upborne with indefatigable wings
Over the vast abrupt . . . ?

None among the choice and prime
Of those Heaven-warring champions could be found
So hardy as to proffer or accept
Alone the dreadful voyage. . . .

—John Milton,
Paradise Lost